GET THE
MOST
FROM YOUR
SEWING
MACHINE

Marion Elliot

D&C
David and Charles
www.rucraft.co.uk

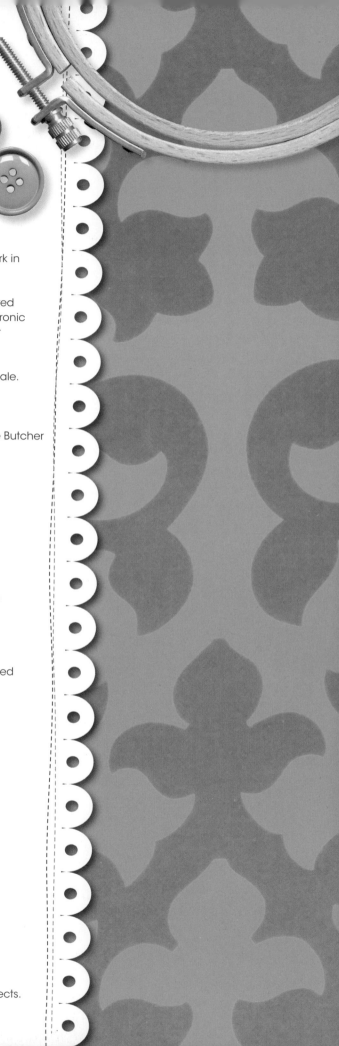

For my mum, Lily Elliot, who taught me how to sew.

A DAVID & CHARLES BOOK
Copyright © David & Charles Limited 2010

David & Charles is an F+W Media Inc. company
4700 East Galbraith Road, Cincinnati, OH 45236

First published in the UK and US in 2010

Text copyright © Marion Elliot 2010

Marion Elliot has asserted her right to be identified as author of this work in accordance with the Copyright, Designs and Patents Act, 1988.

All designs by Marion Elliot except
Purse and bag projects, p21, and bag, p63, by Sally Southern
Star appliqué, p59, Acorn bag, p65, and Heart appliqué, p79, by Alice Butcher and Ginny Farquhar
Knitted bag, p65, by Claire Crompton
Jar covers, p100, Helen Philipps

All photography by Lorna Yabsley except
Cutouts, Karl Adamson
pp21, 63 and 101, Kim Sayer
Artwork, p23, NikolayS
pp59 and 100 Simon Whitmore

A catalogue record for this book is available from the British Library.

ISBN-13: 978-0-7153-3630-4 paperback
ISBN-10: 0-7153-3630-4 paperback

Printed in China by RR Donnelley
for David & Charles
Brunel House, Newton Abbot, Devon

Publisher Stephen Bateman
Acquisitions Editor Jennifer Fox-Proverbs
Editorial Assistant Jeni Hennah
Project Editor Jo Richardson
Designer Mia Farrant
Photographer Lorna Yabsley
Production Controller Kelly Smith
Prepress Jodie Culpin

David and Charles publish high-quality books on a wide range of subjects.
For more great book ideas visit: **www.rucraft.co.uk**

GET THE MOST!

LIVE IT!

WEAR IT!

LOVE IT!

GET THE MOST!

Whether your sewing machine is an established part of your life, or the latest model and your very first, you'll know how quickly you fall in love. We adore our sewing machines; they are reliable, dependable and always there for us, whether we want to run up a pair of curtains, take up a skirt, or make handcrafted gifts. But like many relationships, there comes a time when you think 'how can I put the spice back into this?', 'how can I recapture that initial excitement?', 'how can we fall in love all over again?'. Well, here's your chance.

No matter what the make or model, your machine is a potential creative playground. Just by changing the foot, experimenting with materials, or doodling with the needle, you'll discover that you can do much more than just stitch. You can produce unique, designer homeware, revamp clothes and outfits, and make your downtime more colourful, fun and sociable. You can do all of this with your sewing machine, and that's just for starters…

Your sewing machine can be the gateway to a world of other crafters, all equally smitten and waiting to share their enthusiasm and skill. Once you begin to experiment and disover the potential, you'll want to create more and more. You may reach the point where you need to source recycled materials, revamp your workspace, or even start selling your wares.

This book is designed to act as a springboard, to supercharge your view of your sewing machine. I'm assuming you know the basics (the machine's manual is a good place to start if not), so I've jumped right in to help you look at your old faithful in a new light. Each project explains what makes the idea special, whether it's the choice of materials, techniques or a combination of the two. I've suggested ways for you to explore further, including photos and swatches to inspire. Look out for boxes that refer you to other parts of the book – often one idea or technique wants to take your hand and excitedly drag you off to meet another! I've even included special features that focus on particular aspects of your machine, from the tiniest stitch to whole world of craft.

You may want to browse through these pages reading snippets and taking inspiration, settle down with a cup of coffee to read a particular feature, or just get in front of your machine and start sewing. But whatever your style, one thing's for sure – you're well on your way to getting the most from your sewing machine!

LIVE IT!

Arty Appliqué

I love my daughter's drawings, as they are so full of expression and vitality, and I bet there are children in your family whose art-work is equally charming in its own unique way. Here, I've taken two of my favourites – a flower and a butterfly – and used them as templates to create a funky appliquéd duvet cover for her bedroom. I've attached the fabric shapes with fusible webbing and machine stitched over the raw edges with zigzag stitch to keep them from fraying.

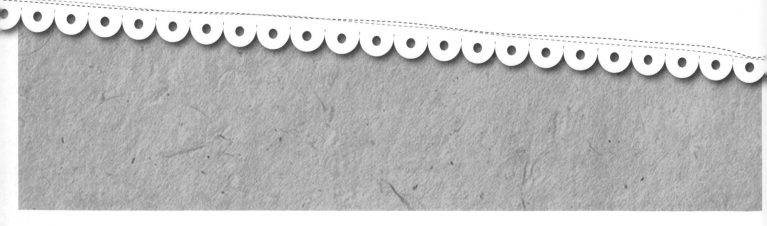

Get into it...

Perfecting your machine appliquéing skills

It's best to use a smallish-sized zigzag stitch for appliquéing the fabric shapes, otherwise the outlines look a little gappy, with too much fabric showing between the stitches. If you've got one, use the see-through appliqué foot, as it makes following the curves of the cut-outs much easier when you can see where you're going!

For more information about the appliqué foot and other useful feet, see pages 40–45.

Sketching with stitches

I've had fun by 'drawing' on details like the leaf veins and the butterfly's wing patterns, body and face with straight stitch in black thread in an imprecise way, to keep the spontaneous feel of the original drawings. Experiment with different sizes of stitch to give a lively effect that works wonderfully well with children's drawings.

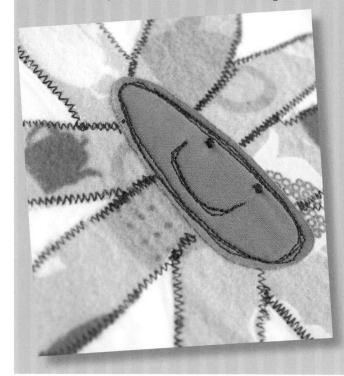

Want to know more about zigzag and other machine stitches? See pages 22–27.

Reusing ready-sewn items

Keen as ever to recycle, I cut a plain cotton sheet in half lengthways to make the front and back of the duvet cover. Once I'd completed the appliqué, I machine stitched the sides and top of the cover together so that the ready-hemmed edges became the lower edge of the cover, to save on sewing time! All I had to do then was add some poppers, or you could use ribbon ties instead for a more 'girly' look.

Mixing it up with pattern

I like to collect together lots of different examples of one kind of pattern, for instance spotted fabric, and combine them in a project. The principle to bear in mind when using any kind of patterned fabric for appliqué is to avoid anything too large or busy, otherwise the appliquéd shape will be too confusing to 'read' and overwhelmed. So instead of giant geometrics or massive florals, look to old patterned 60s and 70s pillowcases and sheets, second-hand dresses and blouses and retro pinnies as sources of patterned fabric.

Mixing it up with textures

I've also tried appliquéing the flower motif in a printed cotton winceyette, with its soft, brushed cotton surface, and you could feature other contrastingly textured fabrics in the design, such as flat cotton combined with needlecord or seersucker. Just remember to use like with like, such as cotton with cotton, so that the cover can be successfully laundered. Always wash and dry all the fabrics first to minimize shrinkage.

- Pencil and tracing paper
- Fusible webbing
- Scissors
- Fabric scraps
- Iron
- Plain cotton sheet for the cover (a single sheet for a young child's duvet or a double sheet for a standard single duvet) and matching thread
- Pressing cloth
- Black thread
- Needle
- Ric rac and matching thread
- Dressmaking pins
- Poppers

1 Trace the different elements of your design, such as the flower head, flower centre, leaf and butterfly used here, onto the paper side of a sheet of fusible webbing. Roughly cut them out. Place the cut-outs, glue-side down, onto your chosen fabrics and iron over the paper to fuse it to the fabric. Cut the cotton sheet in half lengthways.

2 Carefully cut out the shapes, such as the flower head and flower centre, then peel off the backing paper and place them in position, right way up, at the top of one half of the sheet. Continue to transfer, fuse and cut out enough motifs to fit along the top of the front of the cover. Place a pressing cloth over the cut-outs and iron over them to fuse to the fabric.

3 Set your sewing machine to a small zigzag stitch. Carefully sew around the outlines of all the cut-outs with black thread, but leave the inner details unsewn, such as the flower centres and butterfly body in this design.

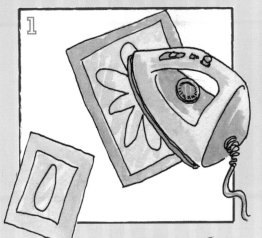

4. Set your sewing machine back to straight stitch. Sew several times around the unsewn parts, such as the flower centres and butterfly body, to make a black outline, sewing in quite a free way so that it almost looks like it's been drawn. Stitched lines have been added in this design to indicate the butterfly's head and across the body.

5. To make flower stems, machine stitch several times up and down below the flower heads. Iron on a pair of leaves below each flower, then outline in straight stitch as before and add veins in the same way. Here, contrasting fabric circles have been ironed onto the butterfly's wings, then outlined and intersecting lines added in straight stitch.

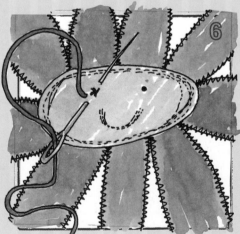

6. To add smiley faces, lightly draw eyes and a mouth in pencil on the motifs and outline them in straight stitch with black thread. You may find it easier to sew in the eyes by hand: make three or four stitches with black thread for each eye. To finish, machine stitch a length of ric rac along the bottom of the design with matching thread. Press the front cover, then pin the front and back cover together with right sides facing. Machine stitch the sides and top edge together, turn right side out and add poppers along the lower, ready-hemmed edge.

Get more...

» When applying appliqué shapes with fusible webbing, use a pressing cloth to protect the fabric surface and the iron. This is because if the gluey paper of the webbing comes into contact with the iron, it will leave a residue on the plate that will mark any other fabric you iron later. Use an offcut of cotton sheeting, or a purpose-designed Teflon® pressing cloth, which is heatproof and transparent so that you can see through to your shapes in order to position them accurately before fusing.

» To save on the cost of using fusible webbing – it's quite expensive – master the art of stitching shapes directly onto a background fabric. You'll need to secure the fabric in an embroidery hoop, stretching it evenly, then drop the feed dogs under the needle before machine stitching around the shapes, which you can keep in place with a pin.

» Add eye interest to your appliquéd shapes with buttons, beads or sequins (see above), although make sure they're washable so that they'll survive repeated laundering. Or outline them with thin braid or ribbon, machine stitched with a medium-length straight stitch.

» You can also add another dimension to your appliquéd designs – literally! – by lightly padding the shapes halfway through attaching them to the background fabric. They can then be machine quilted using straight stitch, hand embroidered or decorated with beads. This effect is especially wowing if metallic fabrics are used.

» Stitch and tear paper is a handy device in appliquéing – a paper that you can draw or write on and then stitch through and tear away. You could use it to incorporate your child's signature into the duvet cover design.

» Get creative with alternative types of fabric and thread that would work well for a particular theme:
• **fairy motifs** or another **fantasy design** would look the part in dreamy sheer fabrics like **organza** or **glitzy metallics**, using a **metallic** or **lurex thread** for the stitching
• **homey gingham** trimmed with **ric rac** and **vintage fabric cut-outs** stitched with **contrasting thread** would make a cute country-style design, as pictured above

See page 27 for some more unusual threads to try.

» Apply your appliquéing skills to making some fun fabric patches – great for transforming holes in jeans into a decorative feature. Simply fuse a fabric shape of your choice onto a slightly larger piece of tough backing material, such as canvas or twill. Machine stitch around the shape with straight stitch and trim away the excess backing fabric, then pin to your chosen item and appliqué in place with zigzag stitch.

Punching Heavy

If you're like me, you'll enjoy nothing better than to chill with a magazine. But as I lie on the couch flicking through one after another, the pile gets taller and taller until I can't ignore it any longer. I'm quite good at stashing magazines away in crates 'for reference', but where to put those I haven't finished with without tripping over them? My solution is this mag store, big and sturdy enough made from oilcloth to take at least six of your favourites, and simple to sew on your machine when you know how.

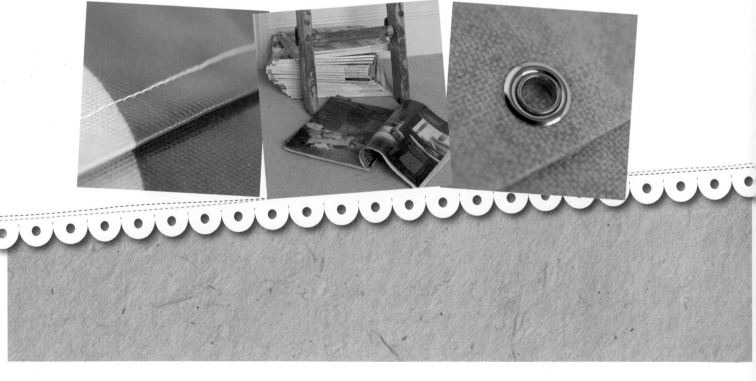

Get into it...

Sewing through oilcloth

This type of fabric can be tricky to sew because it tends to stick to the bottom of your presser foot and the metal throat plate, directly below the needle. However, to ease its passage you can use a plastic Teflon® foot, which glides over the surface of the fabric without sticking to it or puckering it, or a roller foot with rollers that help to move the foot freely over the fabric. If you don't have either feet, place a sheet of tissue paper underneath your oilcloth as you sew, then gently tear it away from the stitches when you've finished. If you're still having problems with puckering, try loosening the tension a bit to give a more even feed through the machine. You'll need to use thicker, stronger machine needles than usual to sew oilcloth; I use denim needles with the usual 100% polyester thread.

For more advice about choosing and using needles and thread, see page 61.

Sourcing oilcloth fabrics

You can buy oilcloth fabric by the metre or yard off the roll, but another good source is plastic tablecloths, which come in lots of exciting colourways and designs – I've used oilcloth intended for tablecloths here. Mexican oilcloth comes in a range of fantastically bold, interesting patterns; look on the internet for suppliers.

Page 81 gives a list of websites that offer examples of fabric designs and inspiration for your sewing projects.

Making the most of your motifs

The retro, stencil-like design of this oilcloth fabric really appealed to me – perfect for bringing a sense of drama to a plain wall. And the individual motifs each define a magazine pocket. But note that the pattern only works in this case because it is exactly aligned on the pockets with the background. So bear in mind that when using any obvious pattern, large or small, you'll need to centre the design on the backing cloth before cutting out the fabric, then cut the pockets to match, allowing for seam allowances and hems.

Keeping in shape

Because the oilcloth I used here is designed for tablecloths, I backed it with reinforced polythene sheeting so that it didn't curl up at the edges (this may not be necessary if you're using very heavy oilcloth). I've also added a sleeve to house a wooden batten top and bottom for the same reason. The ultra-wide polythene sheeting, available from garden centres and hardware stores or builders' merchants by the metre or yard, has a mesh of plastic threads to help prevent it tearing. As the mesh is raised above the surface on one side, it's best to sew it on the other side so that your needle doesn't catch in it.

Get it together...

- 1.5m (1¾yd) of 120cm (48in) wide oilcloth and matching polyester thread
- 1m (1¼yd) reinforced polythene sheeting
- Metal ruler
- Ballpoint pen or pencil
- Scissors
- Low-tack sticky tape
- Five 8mm (⁵⁄₁₆in) diameter metal eyelets and eyelet tools, including tack hammer
- 1.2m (47in) of 3cm (1⅛in) wide wooden batten strip, cut into two equal lengths

1 **For the backing**, cut a piece of oilcloth measuring 100 x 60cm (39¼ x 23½in). Cut a piece of reinforced polythene sheeting to the same size. Use low-tack sticky tape down the sides to hold the two together, then machine stitch around the edges using a 1cm (⅜in) seam allowance. Remove the tape before you sew over it!

2 **For the pockets**, cut three pieces of oilcloth measuring 23 x 60cm (9 x 23½in). Turn under the top and bottom edges by 1.5cm (⅝in). Crease the turned edges to keep them in place, then machine stitch the hems using a 1cm (⅜in) seam allowance. Tape the pockets in position on the front of the backing, the upper pocket 12cm (4¾in) down from the top edge, with the remaining two pockets evenly spaced beneath it. Machine stitch the sides and lower edges of the pockets to secure in place. Remove the tape before you sew over it!

3 Measure the midpoint of each pocket. Machine stitch down the pockets to divide them in half. Remove the tape before you sew over it!

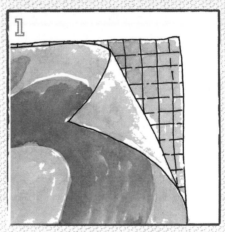
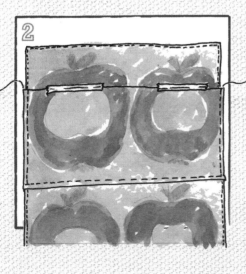
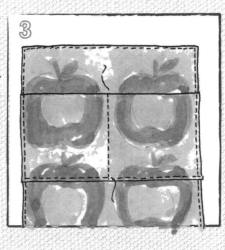

4 Mark the position of the eyelets just below the top edge of the backing, spacing them evenly apart. Fix the eyelets in place according to the manufacturer's instructions.

5 **For the batten sleeves,** cut two pieces of reinforced polythene sheeting measuring 12 x 58cm (4¾ x 22¾in). Fold the sleeves in half lengthways, then machine stitch together along the edge. Machine stitch the sleeves in place at the top and bottom of the backing. Insert a length of batten strip into each.

Get more...

» It's not a good idea to mark seam allowances or fold lines on the front of your oilcloth, as you may not be able to remove the ink afterwards. Instead, make any markings on the back of the fabric with a ballpoint pen or pencil – not a marker or roller ball pen, as the ink may bleed through to the right side of the fabric.

» The reason why I've used tape to hold the pieces of fabric together is that any needle or pinholes you make in your oilcloth will be permanent, so pins are a no-no. I used low-tack masking tape, but you could use plastic electrical tape instead.

For some more tips on sewing with plastics and other unusual materials, see pages 60–65.

» The eyelets fixed along the top edge of the magazine store can be used to hang it from a series of hooks or nails, rather than threading with a length of coloured cord, as pictured on page 17.

» Instead of oilcloth, for alternative effects try using:
• heavy or deckchair canvas
• cotton drill
• sailcloth
• denim

» To make a book or magazine store for a child's room, choose an oilcloth in a specifically girly design or one with obvious boy appeal. Position the store next to a bed, or hang from the end of a set of bunk beds.

» As well as being wonderfully robust, oilcloth is waterproof, so now you know how easy it is to machine stitch, with the right approach, why not use it to run up some bold beach bags, or colourful wash bags to bring a splash of brightness to your bathroom (see left). And any scraps of oilcloth would make a great pencil case or purse (see below).

Turn to pages 86–90 for instructions on how to make a purse using your scrap of oilcloth or any other fabric scraps you may have.

» The size of the magazine store and/or the pockets can be varied to suit other storage purposes:
• one featuring **several smaller pockets** would be ideal for carrying **gardening hand tools** for hanging in a conservatory or shed
• take advantage of its **waterproof** quality and make a **smaller version** with **narrower pockets** for tucking away **bathroom items**

GET THE MOST FROM...

The STITCHES

Even if yours is a very basic sewing machine, the chances are it has a lot more stitch potential than you ever realized. Most people get along quite happily using only two or three stitches, but nearly all machines will have a selection of practical and decorative stitches to explore and have fun with.

Once you've got used to running up and down seams using the standard straight stitch function, start to play around with your machine and graduate to fancier stitches like zigzag and top stitching. You can use all your stitches in a functional or decorative way, so there's lots of scope to experiment.

How does your machine do it?!

No matter which stitch you have, your sewing machine makes it by looping two threads together. One thread comes from a cotton reel at the top of the machine and the other from a small spool called a bobbin that sits immediately below the needle. The upper thread is punched down through the fabric by the needle and loops around the bobbin thread, locking the stitch firmly in place.

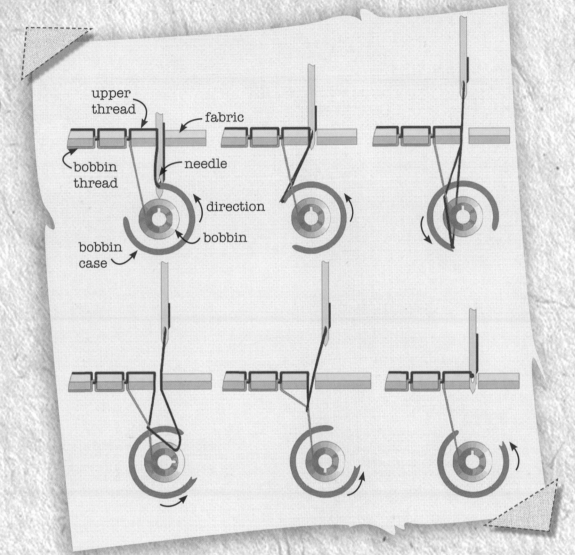

The long and short of it

The fabric is held in position by a presser foot as you sew, and is moved forward by rows of metal teeth – the feed dogs. Setting the stitch length, by turning a dial or pressing a button, controls how the feed dogs move. The teeth grip the fabric and push it through with small movements to make short stitches, or larger ones to make longer stitches.

Stitch length explained

The length of a stitch is measured in terms of millimetres or by the number of stitches per inch. A very short stitch is 0.5mm long, or 60 stitches per inch (spi).

Conversions:

spi	mm	
60	0.5	··················
24	1	····················
13	2	– – – – – – –
9	3	– – – – –
6	4	– – – –
5	5	– – – –
4	6	— — — —

Straight stitch

Your sewing machine will certainly do straight stitch, a very simple stitch that is usually used for making seams. However, it has plenty of practical and decorative uses; as with the simplest things in life, it's dependable, versatile and the one you'll keep going back to.

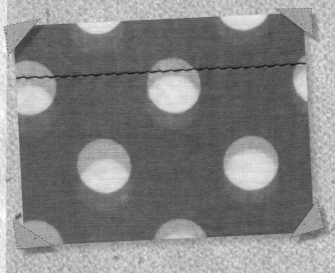

Play with proportion

Usually, you'd use short stitches on small projects such as purses, but using exaggerated, oversize stitches gives a fun, retro result. Be careful if using longer stitches in the constructions, but for decorative features, big stitches in a contrast colour look great.

The baste race

Let's be honest, tacking (basting) – that is, creating long, temporary stitches – can be a necessary evil of sewing, and sewing machine lovers want to avoid hand sewing at all costs. So next time you're faced with miles of hand tacking, just set your straight stitch to its longest length and put your foot to the floor! A 'quick unpick' tool is all you need to remove the machine-basted stitches in a jiffy.

Gather together

Ruffled and gathered fabric looks so pretty, but for a professional finish, the gathering stitch needs to be neat and consistent. A longer-length straight stitch will achieve this in a flash, just leaving it for you to pull up the ends to create perfect folds.

For instructions, tips and ideas on how to create these ruffles and gathers, go to pages 34–38.

Safety first

For extra-secure stitching along seams, bring your stitch length right down for the first and last few stitches when you start and stop. This is especially useful when you don't want to backstitch (maybe the stitching will be seen) or you just want additional security for a project that will be taking lots of strain at the seams.

Getting fancy

These are just some of the stitches you'll find on your machine beyond multi-tasking straight stitch (see opposite). You may have quite a few more, but these are almost universal. All of them will probably have a slightly different version for stretch fabrics, which can be accessed by putting the machine on the stretch stitch setting.

Zigzag stitch

Three-step zigzag stitch

Blind hem stitch with zigzag – for stretch fabrics

Ric rac stitch – used when top stitching

Shirring stitch – used with elastics

Serging stitch – for finishing the edge of stretch fabrics

Reverse stitch – used with stretch fabrics

Stretch stitch

All these stitches have practical applications, but they also make fantastic decorative embroidery effects, especially if you use thread that contrasts with the fabric.

Top stitching

Top stitching is a line, or lines, of stitching that runs parallel to the top of the seam on the right side of the fabric, for example on a pair of jeans. A medium-length straight stitch in heavyweight, contrasting thread is used to add a strong, decorative finish to the seam.

Zigzag stitch

Zigzag stitch is created when the needle swings from side to side as it sews. Another multi-tasker, it is used to neaten raw edges of fabric (appliqué), stop seams fraying (over-locking) and to make buttonholes.

Three-step zigzag

This is a special zigzag that makes three little stitches on each side as it swings from left to right. It makes wide zigzags without puckering the fabric between the stitches.

Three-step zigzag is great for attaching things like ribbon and tape to fabric without puckering. It's also ideal for appliquéing ribbon to fabric. If you use a contrasting thread, the stitching makes a fabulous decorative braid effect along the ribbon.

Blind hem stitch

This is a very useful stitch that saves you spending hours hand sewing hems! On the blind hem setting, your machine will sew a few straight stitches on the pressed-under hem, then swing over to the left to make a single stitch in the main part of the fabric. From the right side of the fabric, these tiny stitches are the only ones that show.

If your machine has blind hem stitch, it will probably have a blind hem foot to let you line up the fabric accurately as you sew. Don't panic if it doesn't, because you can use your basic presser foot instead.

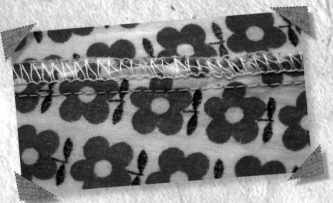

Overlocking stitch

Once you've sewn a seam, you need to do something to the raw edges of your fabric to stop them from fraying. You can sew down each side of the seam allowance using a zigzag stitch, or your machine might have an over-locking stitch specifically for finishing raw edges. Either stitch works well if you sew close to the edge of the fabric, just catching the out-side edge with the top of each stitch.

Free embroidery

You can be fantastically creative if you cover up or lower the feed dogs in your machine. This lets you move the fabric around in any direction under the needle and 'draw' with the needle and thread in a totally free way. Use a darning foot to hold the fabric lightly in place, or remove the foot completely and stitch freestyle – mind your fingers, though, until you've had a lot of practice!

It will be much easier to do free embroidery if you stretch your fabric over an embroidery hoop first. Then you can hold the sides of the hoop and move it beneath the machine to embroider the fabric without puckering it.

Appliqué stitches

One of the decorative techniques I use most of all is appliqué. I assemble a picture from fabric scraps, then sew them to a fabric backing. I attach the scraps to the fabric with an iron-on material known as fusible webbing, then I sew around the shapes with straight or zigzag stitch, usually in contrasting thread for a decorative look.

If you don't want to use fusible webbing, secure the backing fabric in an embroidery hoop and place the appliqué on top before sewing around the edges of the fabric.

Fancy threads to try

Choose your thread according to the weight of your fabric. I use all-purpose polyester cotton thread for nearly everything, but I like thicker threads for top stitching and if I'm using heavier fabrics, such as denim. Other types of thread to try including are:

• Variegated

These threads change colour along the length, adding interest to block-colour fabrics. Choose from a raft of combinations, from subtle earth tones to fun brights.

• Silk

The beautiful sheen of silk thread is most obvious in densely packed stitches, such as a zigzag appliqué stitch.

• Invisible

Yes, really! Made of nylon, this clear thread can be used for any fabrics, although its stiff texture can make it scratchy for clothes. For darker fabrics, a smoky brown shade is available that visually 'melts' into the material.

Clever Quilting

If you've always fancied quilting but find the thought a bit too daunting, here's an ideal project to get you started. I've pieced together strips (or 'blocks' in quilting speak) of lovely soft needlecord and sturdy printed cottons to create a cushioning yet hardwearing mat that also makes a bold style statement, to bring an upbeat note to a bedroom or sitting room. It couldn't be more straightforward to make up, using scraps or odd remnants of fabric, and the quilting process is simplified and speeded up by using a quilting bar attachment on your sewing machine.

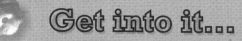
Get into it...

Making light work of quilting

Using a quilting bar is the secret to simple and professional-looking quilting. This metal bar fits onto the back of your presser foot so that you can line it up with the previous row of quilting stitching each time in order to space the quilting lines accurately. And to make things even easier, I've used a ¼in quilting foot, which allows you to sew a row of stitching exactly ¼in (about 5mm) from the edge, or another line of stitching, to sew the blocks together, saving you having to measure and mark a seam allowance.

The ¼in quilting foot is just one of many machine feet you can use to make sewing easy – see pages 40–45.

Getting sassy with sourcing

Washed and worn fabric with its character and softness is just perfect for quilting. Old cotton bed linen, especially winceyette, is comforting to the touch, and also offers the small patterns or prints that are preferable for quilting. Fine needlecord, which I've used here, is also valuable for its velvety texture and durable quality, and can be sourced from old jeans, shirts and, in particular, items of children's clothing, as these tend to have the most individual patterns. Always choose fabrics of equal weight and make sure you wash everything beforehand to avoid problems with shrinkage.

Turn to page 81 for more advice on how to launder and care for your fabric finds.

Perfecting your balancing act

It's important to move all the blocks around and experiment with the composition of your patchwork design before you start sewing them together. If you're unsure where to break up the busyness of the different patterned strips, a good rule of thumb is to add a plain fabric every fourth or fifth block. The plain blocks should contrast or harmonize with the patterns, so pick one of the predominant colours from your main fabrics or choose a complementary for a contrast.

Harmonizing colour and pattern

While the appeal of patchwork is the eclectic mix of colour and pattern, you don't want to end up with a riot on your hands! To achieve unity from all this variation, aim to keep the colour tones even – suddenly throwing a very strong colour into a muted scheme would disrupt the harmony. And keep the different patterns and prints to roughly the same scale, again to avoid individual blocks jumping out and spoiling the overall effect.

Get it together...

- Measuring tape and pencil
- Scissors
- 2.75m (3yd) of 90cm (36in) wide white cotton fabric
- Remnants or scraps of patterned and plain cotton fabrics, and matching and (optional) contrasting thread
- ¼in quilting foot
- Dressmaking pins
- 115g (4oz) cotton wadding (batting)
- Quilt bar
- 50cm (20in) of 115cm (46in) wide plain cotton fabric for the edging and matching thread
- Iron
- Needle

1 **For the mat backing,** cut a piece of white cotton fabric 80 x 130cm (31½ x 51in), plus 5cm (2in) all round. Cut strips of patterned and plain cotton fabric 27cm (10½in) long and in varying widths between 6cm (2⅜in) and 10cm (4in). Attach the ¼in quilting foot to your machine. Pin the long sides of the strips together, right sides facing, and machine stitch. Continue to piece the strips together until you have three lengths long enough to cover the backing fabric.

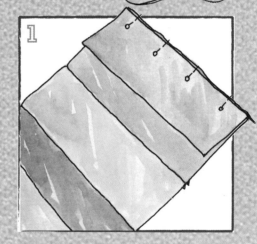

2 Pin together the three lengths of patchwork strips, side by side with right sides facing, to form the mat. Machine stitch the strips together, again using the ¼in quilting foot.

3 Cut a piece of wadding (batting) to the same size as the backing fabric. Place on the backing fabric, then place the mat on top of the wadding (batting), right side up, leaving the 5cm (2in) border all round. Pin and tack (baste) through all layers to secure them together, then machine stitch around the edge of the mat using a 1cm (⅜in) seam allowance. Trim away the excess backing fabric and wadding (batting) from around the mat.

4 To begin quilting the mat, first machine stitch down the three lengths of patchwork strips where they have been sewn together, using either matching thread or a contrasting one, then above and below each individual strip. Use a long straight stitch and follow the seam lines as you sew.

5 Attach the quilt bar to the back of the presser foot and set it to a 5cm (2in) width. Machine stitch down the length of the quilt to make long lines of quilting 5cm (2in) apart.

6 To make the underside of the mat, cut another piece of white cotton fabric slightly larger than the mat. Pin the mat to it, then machine stitch all the way around the edges, using a 1cm (⅜in) seam allowance. Trim away the excess fabric on the underside of the mat.

7 To make the edging, cut two 10cm (4in) wide strips of contrasting plain fabric the same length as the mat. Cut two to the same width, plus 1cm (⅜in) extra at either end. Press under 1.5cm (⅝in) hems down the long edges of all the strips, then press the strips in half. Open out the long strips and pin them, with right sides together, along the long sides of the mat so that the top edge matches the top edge of the mat. Machine stitch in place. Fold the strips over the sides of the mat, then slip stitch in place. Repeat to attach the side strips. Press under the raw edges and slip stitch together.

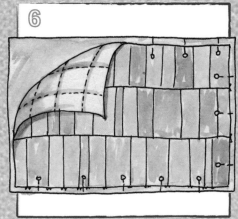

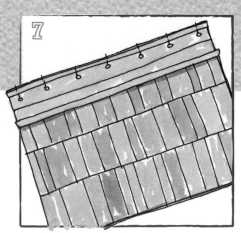

Get more...

» **Don't have a quilting bar?** Simply mark the sewing lines on the front of your fabric with a long ruler and tailor's chalk, which will brush off very easily once you've finished sewing.

» **Don't have a ¼in quilting foot?** It's fine to use the standard one and instead stitch the blocks and patchwork strips together, in Steps 1 and 2, using a 1cm (⅜in) seam allowance – it won't make much difference to the finished size of the mat.

» Make a special keepsake by saving your child's favourite clothes as they grow out of them, cut patches from them and assemble them into a memory quilt. Add a fabric sleeve to the back and insert a length of dowel to hang on the wall. This idea also works well with adults' clothes for a bed quilt, especially brushed cotton men's shirts in checks and stripes.

» Use the basic design of the floor mat to make a beach blanket in bright and breezy stripy cottons and add a waterproof PVA backing. To make it extra sturdy, close quilt it by using your ¼in quilting foot to sew rows of top stitching ¼in (about 5mm) apart. This technique would also be ideal for making a durable beach bag using small blocks of canvas or twill.

» It will probably take you as long to cut out all the pieces of fabric as it will to sew them together! Measure out the blocks on the back of your fabric with a long ruler and ballpoint pen. Don't be tempted to cut more than two layers of fabric at once with scissors, as the fabric is more than likely to slip and your blocks will have wonky edges. However, you can speed up the process by using a rotary cutter that cuts through several layers of fabric at once, available from quilting supply shops or on the internet.

For tips on storing your fabrics and other materials, see pages 100–101.

» Once you've got the quilting plot, there are lots of ways to apply it in different configurations, such as:
• a **diamond pattern** of quilting lines for an **oven mitt** or **tea cosy**
• **close lines** for **place mats** and **coasters**
• **small squares** or **close lines** for a **handbag** (see below)

» I prefer to use cotton wadding (batting) even though it's more expensive than polyester because:
• it's a natural material and is very pleasant to handle
• it's very stable, refusing to bunch up when stitching
• it's fully washable
• it becomes increasingly soft with every wash, so it ages beautifully
• it has far less height (or 'loft', as quilters call it), so doesn't look spongy when quilted, as polyester does
• it shrinks by about 5%, unlike polyester, but even this is an advantage, as it gives a puckered, antique appearance to quilts

Ravishing Ruching

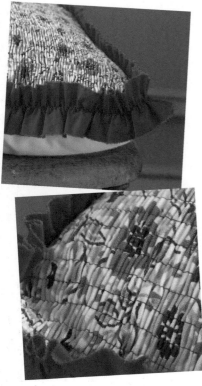

This project features another of my prized flea market finds – a gorgeous linen pinny, still with its intricately woven label intact. Sadly, as with many things of real beauty, it had seen (much) better days, but there was just enough workable fabric left to make a cushion cover. I thought ruching was the perfect decorative treatment – a way of machine gathering using shirring elastic – as that would pull the fabric together and hide all the little flaws. With such a transforming technique, it's easy to see its full creative potential.

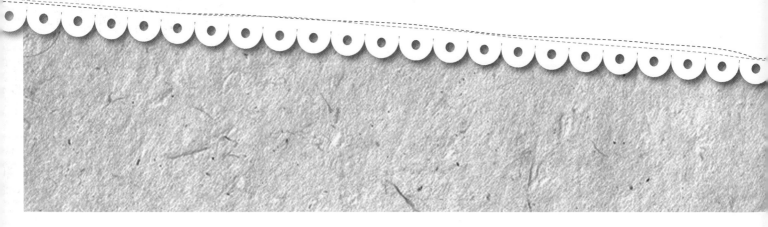

Get into it...

Using shirring elastic

As this is too thick to go through the needle, you need to wind it onto the bobbin of your machine before you begin sewing. Always sew slowly with a fairly long stitch, to get even rows of shirring, and sew from alternate sides at the start of each row to avoid too much fullness at one side of the fabric. Many machines have a shirring stitch, which has a honeycomb pattern and makes broader rows of shirring. A matching thread is often used for ruching, but a strong contrast looks great and emphasizes the technique.

> Find out more about using different machine stitches on pages 22–27.

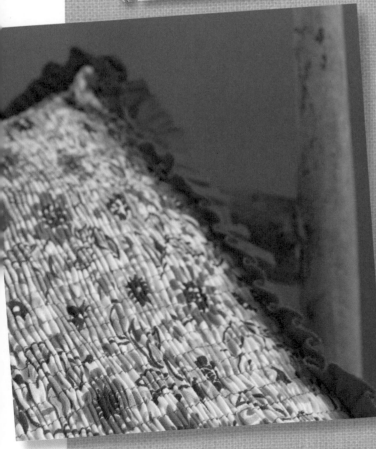

Choosing what's right for ruching

Look for soft fabrics without too much finish in them that drape well, such as old linen, well-washed cottons, winceyette, cotton lawn and soft babycord. The best recycling potential will be offered by large men's shirts and generously sized, loose-fitting dresses and skirts, along with sheets that have interesting patterns – especially ripe for ruching because there's lots of fabric to play with. Many thin, man-made fabrics like nylon satins work well but are not as easy to sew.

> Got the recycling bug? See pages 80–83 for more handy hints.

Thinking big with the small

As ruching is a gathering technique it's preferable to have an ample amount of fabric to work with, but you may well stumble across a special piece of fabric that is small but perfectly formed – as with my precious yet time-punished pinny! But in this case, I only needed to salvage enough fabric to make the front of the cover, since the back is fine made up in plain fabric.

> An even smaller piece of a feature fabric could be used as a ruched panel for a cushion cover.

Teaming ruching with ruffles

The traditional appeal of the fabric and the ruching technique seemed to me best complemented by something in keeping in style. So I trimmed it with a frilly ruffled edging, effortlessly created by machine stitching with shirring elastic down the centre of a fabric strip, which gives a lovely even effect. This is much quicker than the standard gathering method.

- Fine shirring elastic
- Empty bobbin
- Cushion pad, piece of patterned fabric about twice as wide and long as the pad and contrasting thread
- Plain linen fabric for the ruching backing and back of the cushion cover, and matching thread
- Scissors
- Dressmaking pins
- Iron
- Plain cotton or linen fabric for the ruffled edging and matching thread
- Pinking shears
- Needle

1 Carefully wind the shirring elastic onto your empty bobbin spool until the bobbin is almost full. This won't take long, as the elastic is much thicker than thread. Insert the bobbin into the machine and pull up the elastic to the top of the machine, as you would normally do with the bobbin thread.

2 **To begin the ruching,** start at one side of the right side of the fabric, about 2cm (¾in) down from the top edge, and sew a row of stitching to the other side. Sew forwards and backwards a few times at either end to anchor the elastic, and don't sew too quickly. This will gently pucker the fabric. Sew a second row of stitching below the first, lining up the side of your presser foot with the first row as a guide. Continue until the entire piece of fabric is ruched.

3 **For the ruching backing,** cut a piece of plain linen fabric 1.5cm (⅝in) larger all round than the cushion pad. Pin the linen fabric to the reverse of the piece of ruched fabric, stretching the latter gently to fit the linen square. Machine stitch together around the edges, stretching the ruching gently as you sew and using a 1cm (⅜in) seam allowance. Trim away the excess ruched fabric if necessary.

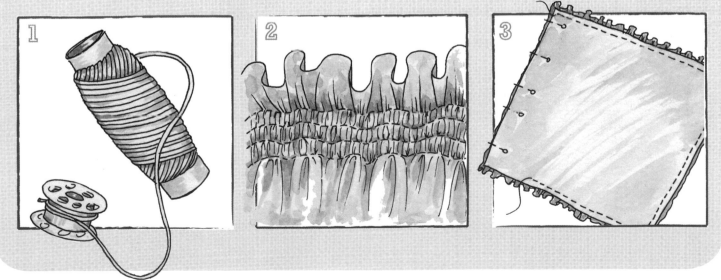

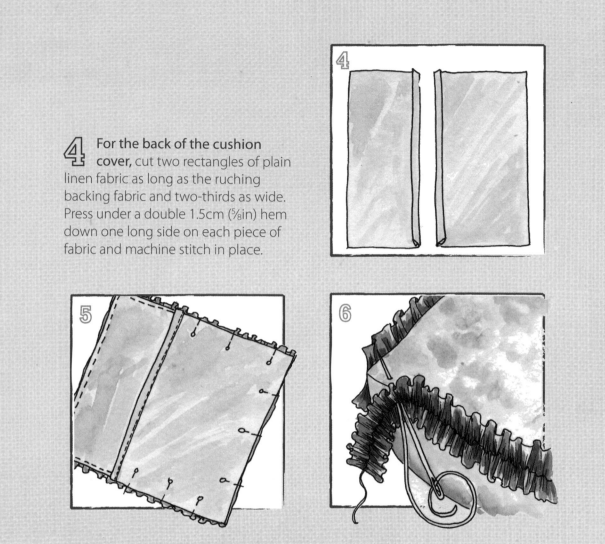

4 **For the back of the cushion cover,** cut two rectangles of plain linen fabric as long as the ruching backing fabric and two-thirds as wide. Press under a double 1.5cm (⅝in) hem down one long side on each piece of fabric and machine stitch in place.

5 Pin one back piece to the front of the ruched fabric, right sides together, stretching it gently to fit. Machine stitch together, stretching it gently as you sew and using a 1.5cm (⅝in) seam allowance. Repeat to add the second back piece, overlapping the hemmed edges at the centre. Trim the corners and turn through. Insert the cushion pad.

6 **To make the ruffled edging,** cut 4cm (1½in) wide strips of plain cotton or linen fabric and join together to make one continuous strip, approximately 1.5m (1¾yd) long. Trim the edges with pinking shears to prevent fraying. Again using shirring elastic in your bobbin and matching thread, machine stitch along the centre of the right side of the strip. Pin the ruffled strip around the edge of the cushion, matching the centre of the strip with the seam line. Hand stitch in place, taking care not to catch the pad as you sew.

Get more...

» Don't worry if you run out of elastic in the middle of a row. Tie off the loose ends on the back of the fabric if you can, then refill the bobbin and machine stitch forwards and backwards a couple of times before you continue sewing.

» Linen usually ruches beautifully, but if your ruched fabric is looking a bit flat, soak the finished cushion cover in water, dry it naturally and press gently with an iron to emphasize the folds.

» Here's another way of enhancing your ruching if the effect looks a little too subtle. When you've finished sewing, spray the ruched fabric with steam from a hot iron, which will shrink the fabric up into the gathers.

For instructions on how to make a corsage using the standard gathering method, see page 58.

» Instead of trimming your ruched cushion cover with ruffled edging, use the same gathering technique to create a frilly corsage from fabric strips, with a button centre, for old-style glam appeal (see above).

» Once you've mastered the art of ruching, use it to make other creative accessories for your home and (favourite) person, such as:
• a ruched fabric **lampshade**
• a gorgeous ruched **handbag** or **clutch** – perfect for a special gift
• a **hairband**, using just a simple strip of ruched fabric
• a ruched **bodice** for a little girl's dress (see left)

» For a vintage look, apply the ruching treatment to old embroidered tablecloths, especially soft, unbleached linen examples. They wouldn't need all-over ruching either – just sew a few rows for a subtle effect.

» Ruching details can be added to all sorts of fabric items as a decorative finishing touch:
• a **couple of ruched rows** along the top of **skirt pockets**
• a **skirt hem** with a **narrow ruched trim**
• a **throw** edged with **ruched narrow cotton tape**

Looking for vintage fabrics? See page 81 for sourcing tips.

GET THE MOST FROM...

The FEET

Sewing machine feet hold the fabric flat and guide the needle while you stitch. There are loads of feet available for lots of different jobs, and the snazziness of your machine will determine how many feet are supplied with it. But don't worry if yours only has two or three – the manufacturer will sell a wide range of feet separately.

You can do an awful lot with the basic presser foot that comes as standard with each machine. In fact, you can do so much with it that you may not have considered trying out all the other feet your machine may have come with. Specific feet are designed for particular tasks, such as inserting a zip, spacing lines of stitching accurately or stitching close to the edge of the fabric. Knowing what each foot does will make jobs like hemming and overlocking much more simple to do, and will enable you to achieve a better finish as well as get maximum fun out of using your machine.

So how do you change your feet?

Traditionally, the foot is attached to the sewing machine by a large screw behind the needle, which holds the foot very securely but makes changing feet more of a task. However, many modern machines now have snap-on feet, which you clip on and off the machine with a small lever. I prefer these because they're easier to change, but they're less secure and do drop off occasionally in the middle of a seam!

Get familiar with your feet

The following are the sewing machine feet that you'll come across most often:

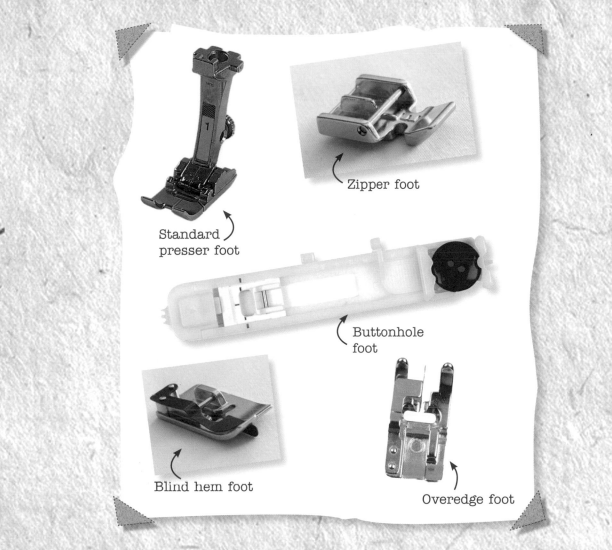

Standard presser foot

Zipper foot

Buttonhole foot

Blind hem foot

Overedge foot

Standard presser foot

This is the foot that you'll probably use most of all when sewing. It's an all-purpose foot used for sewing straight stitch. It has a wide slot that allows the needle to swing from side to side to sew zigzag stitch too. It is also used for doing more complex functional and decorative stitches.

It's meant for Straight and zigzag stitch
But try it for Fantastic decorative stitching

Zipper foot

This foot has a long, narrow 'toe' at the front, which allows you to position the foot as close to the zip teeth as possible while sewing. Zipper feet are also very useful for inserting piping, sewing on pockets, top stitching or anything else that requires a narrow or close seam. Some machines also have a special zipper foot that is specifically for inserting invisible zips into seams.

It's meant for Inserting zips
But try it for Making and inserting piping, sewing on pockets, top stitching or anything else that requires a narrow or close seam

Overedge foot

This foot is is the domestic equivalent of an industrial overlocker. It's used in conjunction with the overlocking stitch to create a very sturdy line of stitching along the raw edges of the seam allowance to stop the fabric from fraying and unravelling (see page 26). It's also great for creating decorative stitching.

It's meant for Finishing seam edges
But try it for Adding decorative details to fabric

Buttonhole foot

Your machine may have a manual or automatic buttonhole function. Manual buttonholes are made in up to four steps, with a standard presser foot or sliding buttonhole foot. Automatic buttonholes are made with an automatic buttonhole foot, which moves itself across the fabric, creating perfect buttonholes in one step. These feet often have a button gauge too, which automatically measures the size of the button before making a buttonhole to just the right size. Buttonholes can also be worked vertically as carriers for ribbon.

It's meant for Making buttonholes
But try it for Making slots for ribbon

Blind hem foot

This foot is used in conjunction with blind hem stitch (see page 26) to make an (almost) invisible hem. It has an extending gauge that butts up against the hem as you work, allowing you to sew a neat and accurate hemline. It's most often used on garments and when hemming large items such as curtains where a professional finish is important. The foot is also good for sewing on ribbons and bias binding, and blind hem stitch can be used to sew decorative details onto fabric.

It's meant for Sewing blind hems
But try it for Sewing on ribbons and bias binding; adding decorative details to fabric

Appliqué foot

This is a very useful, clear plastic version of the standard presser foot so that you can see where you're going when you're sewing appliquéd shapes. I also use it for sewing curved shapes as well as for quilting and creating decorative stitching.

It's meant for Appliqué
But try it for Sewing curved shapes; quilting; adding decorative stitching

Teflon® foot and roller foot

The Teflon® foot is coated in plastic and glides more easily over synthetic fabrics than the standard metal presser foot. It's especially useful when sewing with heavy-duty plastic fabrics, such as oilcloth (see pages 16–21 and 64). The roller foot is also great for controlling materials that are difficult to feed through the machine, having two textured rollers that help move the foot freely over leather, suede, velvet and vinyl.

Satin stitch foot

This foot is another useful tool if you're doing appliqué. It creates a line of very close zigzag stitches with a satiny appearance, and gives a denser outline than ordinary zigzag stitch.

Feet for thought

Here are some fabulous feet that probably won't come with your machine, but when you know what amazing things they can do, you'll wish they did!

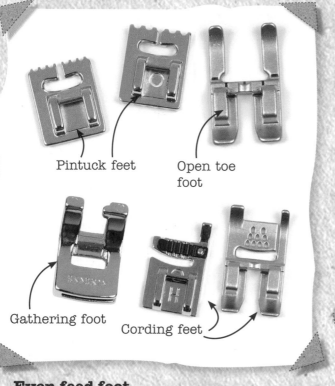

Pintuck feet

Open toe foot

Gathering foot

Cording feet

Even feed foot

First up is a very clever and hardworking foot that comes with its own set of feed dogs to help the flow of fabric through your sewing machine. It makes sewing through heavy fabrics and thick layers a breeze, because it feeds the top fabric through at the same speed as the machine's feed dogs, so there's no pulling or puckering. It's really handy when you're quilting through layers or sewing fabrics with a pile that might stick, such as velvet or suede.

Cording foot

Next up is this very nifty little foot, which has one or more central grooves that you can feed through cord and elastic, before they're automatically overstitched in place with a zigzag stitch casing. You can also use the cording foot with a double needle for threading with yarn and threads, which can be overstitched for a very pretty effect.

Gathering foot

This is a great invention that gathers up the fabric while you sew, creating perfect shirring without the need for elastic. The gathering foot is ¼in, or about 5mm, wide, so you can use the edge as a guide to make rows of stitching exactly ¼in (5mm) apart. You can change the fullness of the gather by the length of stitch you use; the longer the stitch, the fuller the gather.

¼in quilting foot

This foot measures exactly ¼in, or about 5mm, from the needle to the right-hand edge of the foot, enabling you to sew perfect ¼in (5mm) seams and rows of top stitching. It's very popular with quilters because it makes piecing sections of patchwork ultra speedy, dispensing with the need for all that time-consuming measuring.

Open toe foot

This highly useful, versatile foot is a favourite for machine embroidery because it has a wider than usual channel at the front of the foot so that you get a really good view of where you're about to sew. This is very helpful if you've got markings or designs to follow on your fabric.

Pintuck foot

Another funky foot that works with twin needles, the pintuck automatically creates small tucks in the fabric as you sew. It has a grooved underside that helps to form the tucks and ensures that they're evenly spaced. You'll need to tighten the upper thread tension to pucker your fabric into tucks, then the twin needles sew a line of stitching at either side of the tuck to keep it in place.

Darning foot

This is a handy little number because it does so much more than darn. Its main purpose is to hold hooped fabric lightly in place and stop it puckering while you stitch over holes and tears. But the task I like to use it for most is free machine embroidery. It keeps everything together and stops your fabric puckering and pulling, yet it's so unobtrusive, lets you see exactly what you're doing and gives you lots of freedom to whizz over the surface of your fabric in a creative frenzy!

Ruffler foot

One of the most impressive feet, the ruffler automatically makes pleats or gathers in your fabric. It's such a clever bit of kit that it can also attach ruffles to a second piece of fabric as it gathers, cutting down hugely on the amount of work that you have to do. Plus it's incredibly easy to use: you simply set it to the amount of fullness or size of pleats you want, then feed through your fabric and the foot does the rest.

Ribbon and sequin foot

Last but not least, this ingenious foot has an adjustable front opening that allows you to feed through ribbon or strung sequins as you sew. The foot keeps the ribbon or sequins flat and feeds them through at an even rate, which makes for a neater, more accurate result than using the standard presser foot.

Corsage Craft

Corsages are such a creative way of bringing a splash of colour to any outfit. In fact, every girl should have several, and little girls will love them especially. This one has a buttonhole in the centre, so you can simply and securely attach it to any button you like – perhaps at the top of a child's dress, to a jacket lapel or on a hat. Corsages are wonderfully quick and easy to make, and are great for using up odd scraps of interesting, vibrant fabrics.

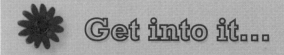

Get into it...

Playing with pattern

Here, I have majored on one type of pattern – spotty – but have chosen a range of different styles and sizes of spot. This gives the design lots of visual interest, but also provides a link between the various fabrics to make a satisfying whole. Plus I have subtly varied the textures, using a mixture of cottons and linens.

Stitching for fun

I have outlined the petals of the flower as well as the flower centre with lines of machine stitching, sewn in a deliberately imprecise way using a sharply contrasting thread for each different fabric. This brings a fun, spontaneous feel to the corsage and loosens up its bold, graphic form.

Choosing your colour scheme

As this design is for a child, I opted for bright, zany colours to accentuate its cartoony appeal and to tie in with the free and lively stitching. But you could easily create very different effects by using alternative palettes – earthy tones in wools or tweeds, or soft, dusty hues mixed with subtle patterns in brushed cotton or needlecord.

Brushing up on buttonholing

I used my machine to make the buttonhole centre for the corsage the quick and easy way. Some machines come with an automatic or one-step buttonhole function, while others have a manual or four-step function. If your machine has automatic buttonholing, it will come with a special buttonhole foot that will measure the button and sew a buttonhole to the right length. If it doesn't, to make the right length of buttonhole, add 5mm (¼in) to the length of your button. To cut open the buttonhole (some machines will do it for you!), starting at the middle, snip slowly and carefully with your scissors to the ends, or use a seam ripper to cut through the fabric with great care.

Curious to know what those other mysterious attachments for your machine do? All is revealed on pages 40–45.

- Pencil and thin paper
- Fusible webbing
- Scissors
- 7 scraps of different patterned fabrics and 1 scrap of plain, and contrasting thread
- Iron
- Scraps of sturdy backing fabric
- Pressing cloth
- Pinking shears
- Buttonhole foot (optional)
- Seam ripper (optional)

1 Transfer the petal template (page 124) seven times onto the paper side of a sheet of fusible webbing. Roughly cut them out. Place the cut-outs, glue-side down, onto seven scraps of patterned fabric and iron over them to fuse them to the fabric. Remove the backing paper and place them on scraps of backing fabric. Place a pressing cloth over the cut-outs and iron over them to fuse them to the fabric and make them more substantial.

2 Machine stitch around each petal several times in a fairly free way, using contrasting thread and a medium straight stitch, to keep the layers together and to create a decorative effect. Trim around each petal with pinking shears.

3 Transfer the flower centre template (page 124) twice onto the paper side of fusible webbing. Roughly cut them out and place them, glue side down, onto a scrap of plain fabric. Iron over them to fuse them to the fabric. Cut them out. Remove the backing paper and lay one flower centre, glue-side up, on your work surface. Arrange the petals around the centre to form the flower.

4 Place the second flower centre in the middle of the flower, glue-side down, overlapping the base of the petals. Place a pressing cloth over it and iron over it to fuse the two flower centres together.

5 Machine stitch around the flower centre several times with contrasting thread to keep all the layers together. Set your machine to the buttonhole function and attach a buttonhole foot if you have one. Sew a buttonhole in the middle of the flower centre to fit your button. Cut a slit in the buttonhole using a seam ripper, if your sewing machine isn't able to do this automatically.

Get more...

» Use a see-through buttonhole foot if you have one – it makes it much easier to judge when you've reached the end of the buttonhole!

» Making the corsage with a particular outfit in mind? Pick three or four colours that feature in it and use them to form the basis of your colour scheme. You could also choose complementary colours for a high-impact effect.

» Instead of using straight machine stitching, try sewing different decorative machine stitches around the petals. Or embellish the petals with simple embroidery stitches, hand stitched in contrasting thread, such as running stitch, chain stitch or feather stitch. You could also work in some translucent or pearlized sequins or seed beads as you sew, for extra glitz.

> If you want to find out more about fancy machine stitches, go to pages 25–27.

» Use a loose-woven fabric to make the petals, so that once they are stitched you can fray the edges for an alternative decorative effect.

» Worried that your chosen fabrics are too flimsy for your corsage? Sew them onto several layers of sturdy fabric first, to give them some 'body'. Woollen fabrics and felts make excellent backing material because they pad out the corsage without making it too stiff (see above).

» Reduce the size of the templates to make smaller flowers and turn them into brooches by sewing a safety pin or brooch fastening to the back, as I did with the one above left. Use other fun motifs, such as cupcakes or teacups, hearts, butterflies or birds.

» Create cool patches for clothing and accessories using the basic corsage shape. Make up the flower as usual but omit the buttonhole (see above). Then pin it where you want it and hand stitch in place.

On-trend Trimming

Got an old jacket that's in good condition but looks rather tired, sad and outdated? Here's a speedy way to groove it up with the minimum of fuss using simple sewing techniques. I've sewn a trim of contrasting narrow cotton tape all the way around the edges of the jacket to make it look more like a blazer, so that I can wear it with jeans and other casual clothes, and replaced the original buttons with more eye-catching examples. And to enhance it's style and cut, I've added a half belt to the back of the jacket.

Get into it...

Building on quality

If you're starting from scratch rather than recycling one of your old jackets, look for one that has a good cut and decent fabric – check out the label for details and also see how it hangs – in an attractive, plain colour. However hard you try, you can't transform a poor-quality item into a designer piece. Scour charity shops and markets for great bargains, like the jacket I've used here. It's made from pure wool, is in great condition and cost me next to nothing.

Like the idea of recycling and revamping second-hand finds? See pages 80–83 for further inspiration.

Investing in the detail

If you're either making-over your own jacket, and therefore saving money on not buying a new one, or you've managed to pick one up for a song, you can afford to go to town on the added detailing. This way you'll get designer looks for a fraction of designer prices! Take time to find buttons and trimmings that really work with the colour and texture of your jacket fabric, looking for striking colour combinations, such as the textured, oversize wooden ones I found, which complement the cotton tape trim. But also make sure that any trimming and contrasting fabrics are all washable at the same temperature as your jacket, and if you choose unusual buttons, you may need to remove them before laundering.

Putting on the style

I enhanced the character of my jacket by sewing on a half belt to the back, which gives it a more tailored look by cinching in the waist a little. And instead of going for a coordinating fabric, I chose a patterned tweed to add a flash of unexpected colour. I used the same fabric to fashion a corsage for the lapel, with a button centre that echoes the bold buttons used on the front and back of the jacket. These are the all-important design details that will make your jacket stand out from the crowd.

Keep the original jacket buttons if you like them for another sewing project.

Keeping it simple

I've used basic sewing techniques only for this project, but executed on the machine they produce sophisticated results. Again, the zipper foot, which comes as standard with almost all machines, proves its worth by enabling you to sew as close as possible to the edge of the tape used to trim the edges of the jacket. And simple straight stitch on the machine's longest setting is all you need to sew along a strip of hemmed fabric in order to pull the threads and gather it into a crafty corsage!

If you want to know more about what your zipper foot can do for you, see page 42.

1. Press under one end of the cotton tape. Position the tape around the edges of your jacket, about 3mm (⅛in) from the folded edge, and tack (baste) it in place. Tack (baste) tape around the lower edges of the sleeves and along the pocket openings too. Using the zipper foot on your machine and matching thread, very carefully machine stitch the tape in place, as close to the edge of the tape as you can. Remove the original buttons from your jacket and sew on replacement buttons in the same position, using contrasting button thread.

2. **To make the half belt,** cut a piece of contrasting fabric 13cm (5in) wide and long enough to fit across the back panel of your jacket, adding 3cm (1⅛in) for turnings. Fold the fabric in half, with right sides together, and machine stitch around the edges using a 1.5cm (⅝in) seam allowance, leaving a 10cm (4in) gap along the lower edge to turn through. Turn the belt through and slip stitch the opening closed. Press. Pin and tack (baste) the half belt in position on the back of your jacket. Machine stitch down the short sides to secure in place. Sew a large button at either end of the half belt.

- Old jacket
- About 3.5m (4yd) of 1cm (⅜in) wide cotton tape (for a medium-sized jacket) and matching thread
- Iron
- Tacking (basting) cotton and needle
- Scissors
- Buttons and contrasting button thread
- Scraps of contrasting fabric and matching thread
- Dressmaking pins
- Needle
- Scrap of felt
- Small safety pin

3 **To make the corsage,** cut a strip of contrasting fabric measuring 30 x 7cm (12 x 2¾in). Press under and machine stitch 1cm (⅜in) hems all the way around the sides of the strip. Change your stitch length to the longest setting and machine stitch along the top edge of the strip. Sew backwards and forwards a couple of times at the start, but leave the threads free at the other end. Pull up the free ends of the thread to gather the fabric.

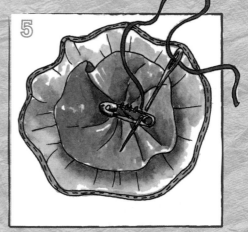

4 Continue to pull the threads up so that the strip forms a rosette shape. Hand stitch the threads into the end of the strip a few times to keep them in place, then slip stitch the edges of the strip together where they overlap.

5 Cut a circle of felt about 1cm (⅜in) smaller all round than the corsage and sew it to the back of the corsage. Sew a safety pin to the felt to make a fastening. Sew a button to the front of the corsage as decoration.

Get more...

» Want your jacket to look really neat on the inside? Carefully unpick the stitching along the lower edge of the lining and pull it up out of the way before you sew on the half belt, so that you don't stitch through the lining. Then neatly slip stitch back in place.

» Don't just stick to traditional jackets when you're planning to revamp your wardrobe. Buttons and trims have such great powers of transformation that skirts, shirts, cardigans and trousers will all benefit from a bit of their makeover magic.

» Instead of using flat ribbon or braid for trimming, try:
• **miniature bobble fringing** to create an unusual effect around **cuffs** and along **pocket edges**
• **beaded trim**
• **fringed woollen braid** – great with **tweeds**
• extra **strips** of the **contrasting tweed ruffled** on the machine with **shirring elastic** for sewing around **cuffs**

For instructions on how to use shirring elastic to ruffle a fabric strip, see pages 36–37.

» Instead of trimming with tape, add some simple machine embroidery to the pockets – you'll need to unpick them and then re-attach after stitching – and/or the lapels.

» Other good combos of fabrics and trims are (see below):
• **tweed** with richly coloured **velvet ribbon**
• **denim** with **narrow satin ribbon**
• **corduroy** and **baby cord** with **cotton tape** or bias binding
• **heavy cottons** with **woven braids**

See page 25 for some samples of fancy stitching you can do on your machine.

» **Want to jazz up your jacket more?** Add some appliqué in contrasting fabric. Simply attach your cut-outs with fusible webbing and machine stitch around the edges using a clear appliqué foot (see above). Unpick the lower edge of the lining to avoid stitching through it.

» **Found two jackets that you really like?** Consider swapping the pockets to make an interesting design detail.

» **Found a lovely jacket that's too big?** Use the half belt feature to gather in some of the fullness at the back, making it narrower than the back panel.

» **Want another quick way to enhance or update an old jacket?** Try reworking an extra buttonhole on your machine to raise the neckline.

GET THE MOST FROM...

Different MATERIALS

The world's your oyster when it comes to machine sewing. Materials that would be very tiring to sew by hand can be whizzed through a machine in minutes, and this gives you plenty of scope to look beyond cotton fabrics to paper, card, leather and plastics, as well as the more usual velvets, satins and knits. As long as you use the right kind of needle, the right stitch and the right thread, you'll be able to sew lots of different types of material that you didn't think possible, as well as some you did but were afraid to try.

The best way to find out what works with different materials is to experiment first. Cut a swatch and sew slowly up and down a few times to see if your machine's tension and stitch length work; then adjust them if necessary before you use up your precious stock.

Needle know-how

Machine needles come in lots of different widths and sizes, so it's important to choose the correct one for the material you are sewing. Needles are designed for specific weights of fabric; for example, a very fine fabric requires a fine needle, and something heavy like denim will need a much sturdier needle.

Whichever needle you're using, remember to change it every time you start a new project, as they do blunt fairly quickly, especially with more unusual materials like paper and plastics. If you find your fabric puckers even with a new needle, it probably means that the one you're using is too thick, so switch down a size and see if that helps. For a really smooth finish, remember to use a shorter stitch for fine fabrics and a longer stitch for thick ones.

Needle sizes and types explained

Needles are gauged by thickness, for example:

Size 60(8) very thin; used for delicate fabrics like chiffons, voiles and fine silks
Size 80(11) a good all-rounder, perfect for medium-weight fabrics
Size 110(18) the thickest; used for fabrics such as denim and canvas

Within this range of sizes, you'll find needles with different tips, according to the kind of fabric you're sewing:

Ballpoint needles for stretch fabrics; they pierce the fabric without cutting the fibres
Sharps for woven fabrics
Wedge- or chisel-points for leathers and heavier fabrics; they slice through the material

So which thread?

You will be faced with a very wide choice of threads when you start sewing. As a general rule, polyester thread is a good all-rounder suitable for sewing most materials. However, you may like to stick to the traditional guidelines and choose natural threads for natural fabrics: cotton for cottons, and silk for silks and wools. Polyester thread is fine for synthetics, plastics and leather.

Sewing with paper

Besides sewing with thread in the usual way, you can also use your machine without a top thread or bobbin thread to create a pricked paper effect, making delightfully delicate patterns formed from lines of perforated holes. This technique is great for small-scale projects such as greeting cards, or use it on a larger scale for making a lampshade.

thread Cotton and polyester threads both work well when sewing paper.
needle Use a fine needle, size 60(8)–70(9), and a long stitch, and sew slowly for best results and to avoid damaging the paper.
stitches Straight stitch is great for general sewing on paper (see page 24), while zigzag, blind hem, overlocking and most stretch stitches work well for decorative effects (see pages 25–26). Avoid dense stitches like satin stitch – they tend to pucker or tear the paper.

Technique tips

• Once you stitch your paper, the holes are permanent and will be difficult to hide, so plan where you're going to sew first.

• If your paper is very thin, sew it to a heavier sheet of backing paper first, or the feed dogs may tear it as you stitch. You can stitch fairly heavy paper quite easily with a machine, but I don't use anything thicker than watercolour paper, because it blunts the needles too quickly.

Sewing with leather and suede

You may find working with these materials a little daunting at the outset, so start with a simple strap for a bag – maybe recycled from an old belt – and then as your experience and confidence grows you can tackle making a whole leather or suede bag.

thread Polyester thread is suitable for sewing leather and suede, and far more durable than cotton, which tends to rot.
needle Although they will work quite well with suede, normal sewing machine needles will not be sharp enough to pierce leather and will break very easily, so use leather needles, which have very sharp, blade-like points that cut cleanly through the material.

Sewing with plastics

These waterproof materials give you plenty of scope for making a range of practical accessories and clothes. Try sewing up some simple tote bags for your friends — they make ideal stocking fillers at Christmas. An apron is another easy project to begin with, from which you can build up to making a raincoat or hat for a small child.

stitches Use a medium-long stitch and sew slowly; a short stitch will make too many needle holes close together, resulting in perforated edges that tear easily.

Technique tips

• Don't make markings on the right side in case they show. Draw your cutting lines and seam allowances on the back with a ballpoint pen or fabric marker before you begin.

• Dressmaking pins are a no-no for leather and suede, as they permanently mark and distort the surface. A good alternative is leather tape, which holds everything together while you work. Also try clothes pegs or low-tack paper tape, but test on a scrap first to make sure they don't leave a mark.

• A rotary cutter will cut through leather and suede quickly and smoothly without leaving jagged edges, and saves a lot of hard work!

• Use a Teflon® foot or roller foot when sewing leather, as it will glide over the material much more smoothly than a metal presser foot (see page 43). If you're still having problems, dust the surface of the leather with a little talcum powder.

• Remember that needle holes will be permanent, so plan exactly where you're going to sew before you start.

thread Polyester thread works very well when sewing with plastics.
needle Use denim needles, but you might like to try leather needles too if your material is particularly thick.
stitches Use a medium-long stitch to avoid stitching rows of perforations, as with leather.

Technique tips

• Make all your sewing and cutting markings on the back of the material with a ballpoint pen or pencil. Don't use a marker or roller ball pen, as the ink may bleed through to the right side.

• Use a Teflon® foot if at all possible, which glides over the surface of the plastic much more easily than a metal presser foot, or a roller foot (see page 43). If you haven't got either, try dusting the plastic with a little talcum powder and placing a sheet of tissue paper between your plastic material and the throat plate (directly under the needle). Sew through all layers as normal, and once you've finished, tear off the excess paper from the line of stitching.

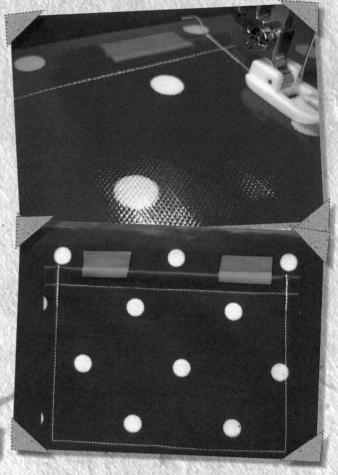

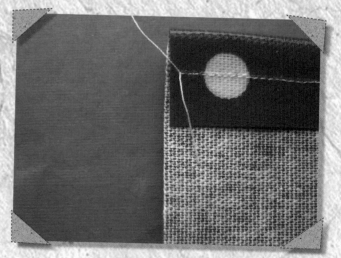

• Don't stitch backwards and forwards at the start of each row, or you may tear the material. Instead, pull the top thread through to the back with the bobbin thread and tie off the ends at the back.

• As with leather and paper, any needle or pinholes you make in plastics will be permanent, so don't use pins to keep layers together as you sew. Use low-tack masking tape or plastic electrical tape; avoid sticky tape and parcel tape, as they leave behind a messy residue. Also very useful are small bulldog clips or clothes pegs.

Sewing with other tricky fabrics

Don't shy away from using other challenging fabrics including woollens and silks, synthetics and stretch fabrics as well as fabrics with a pile, as they can all be sewn on your sewing machine with a little extra care and attention and made into out-of-the-ordinary home or fashion accessories.

Wool and silk fabrics

These natural materials should ideally be sewn with silk thread, because it disappears into the surface and becomes barely visible. Silk tends to be slippery and difficult to sew, but placing tissue paper under the fabric and using a fine needle does help to pass it smoothly through the machine as it stitches. Knitted wool fabric stretches, so turn your dial to the stretch stitch setting before starting to sew, and use a ballpoint needle. Old woolly jumpers can be shrunk on a hot machine wash and then cut up to make interesting cushions, purses and bags.

Synthetic, shiny and stretchy fabrics

These are difficult to cut and sew neatly, but if you love the fabric and bring patience and care to bear, the end results will be worth it. Placing the fabric on an old sheet or length of cotton fabric is useful when you are cutting out, because it helps to stop the fabric sliding around. Very fine, silky fabrics should be sewn with a fine needle to prevent them from puckering. Try using scraps of showy synthetic fabrics to make luxurious evening bags or purses. Stretchy fabrics should be sewn slowly and carefully on the stretch stitch setting to prevent distortion. Snazzy snippets of these are perfect for sewing up into i-pod or mobile phone cases that will make great gifts.

For instructions on how to make a purse from a scrap of fabric, see pages 86–91.

Piled fabrics

These fabrics, such as velvet, have a nap, which means that the surface is covered with very short fibres that can be brushed in the right or wrong direction. You need to take care to cut out all the pieces of your project with the nap running in the right direction, or they will look mismatched when sewn together. These fabrics make wonderfully tactile corsages that look especially impressive in dramatic, jewel-like colours.

Turn to page 58 for steps showing you how to make a fabric corsage.

Scrap Style

For those cool teens in your life, here is a trio of stylish accessories made from fabric scraps – easy projects but ones that give you lots of scope for projecting your own personality in the choice of pattern, colour and embellishment. The sequinned cuff is a fun way of featuring a boldly patterned offcut, the oriental-style belt is another perfect opportunity to showcase a striking pattern, while the hairband needs only a smidgen of scrap, salvaged from a favourite but flagging garment, to glam up a plain outfit.

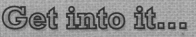

Get into it...

Creating an impact

These projects are all about bringing a touch of individuality to an outfit and making a strong visual statement, so the bolder and more unusual fabrics you choose, the better. I used a scrap of a particularly wacky furnishing fabric for the cuff, which gives it a real edge, while the hairband is made from a snippet of an old yet vibrant summer dress. And the belt features 70s curtain fabric with a repeat pattern of monumental proportions that looks quite intriguing applied to something small scale, and it's heavy, black outlining on a white background has an appropriate oriental feel.

Putting your leftovers to good use

These are ideal items for using up any remnants of fabric left over from a previous sewing project, so rummage through your stash of scraps to see what interesting and bold patterns spring out. And being quick and simple to run up, they make great last-minute gifts. Think about textures too – tactiles such as velvet, silk, wool, tweeds and sari fabrics would all work especially well. Look through your old clothes, or have a hunt through second-hand sources, for items with project potential – an embroidered hem section from a baggy old skirt would make a fab hairband, and there would be enough material in a fake leather or suede jacket to make cuffs for all your friends.

Making a virtue out of necessity

As the design for the obi belt is based on a kimono sash, it's very long, so I've devised the pattern using three different sections so that you can make it up using scraps of fabric. I have used this opportunity to line the back of the side panels of the belt with contrasting plain fabric so that the patterned ties contrast nicely with the lining when they wrap around the waist, giving it an extra dimension of wearability. As an accent accessory, this really will speak volumes!

Having fun with embellishments

I added some decorative detail to finish off the cuff in the form of two rows of pale pink pearlized sequins along the top and a single row of black sequins along the bottom, which both work especially well against the deep pink of the fabric, and complement the button fastening. Look out for buttons with an interesting finish – mother-of-pearl are lovely, as are sparkly, metallic or glass examples. Check out second-hand clothes for button bounty – old cardigans are an especially promising source.

See page 76 for further pointers on sourcing and reusing buttons creatively.

Cutting-edge Cuff

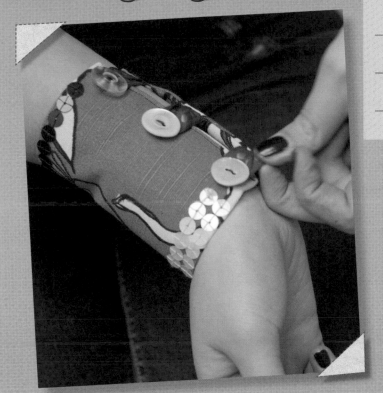

Get it together...

- Scrap of fabric and matching thread
- Scissors
- Fusible interfacing
- Dressmaking pins
- Iron
- 30cm (12in) narrow ribbon
- 3 buttons
- Needle and matching thread
- Sequins

1. Cut a rectangle of scrap fabric 25 x 20cm (10 x 8in). Cut a piece of fusible interfacing 25 x 10cm (10 x 4in), pin to the centre of the wrong side of the fabric and iron in place.

2. Cut three 10cm (4in) lengths of narrow ribbon, fold each in half to form a loop and pin to the right-hand side of the rectangle, one in the centre and the other two either side, 4cm (1½in) from the centre. Fold the fabric in half lengthways, with right sides facing, making sure that the ribbon loops are on the inside. Pin and machine stitch around the sides and lower edge, using a 1cm (⅜in) seam allowance and leaving a 10cm (4in) opening along the lower edge to turn through the cuff.

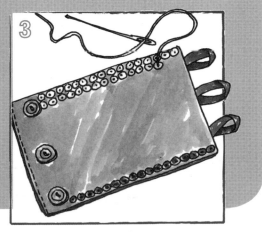

3. Clip the corners, turn the cuff through to the right side and press. Press under the raw edges at the opening and slip stitch the opening closed. Press under the raw edges at the un-looped side and machine stitch closed on the front of the cuff. Wrap the cuff around your wrist and make a pencil mark where each button will go, beneath each loop. Sew on the buttons, then hand sew rows of sequins along the top and bottom edges of the cuff.

Awesome Obi Belt

Get it together...

- Thin paper and pencil
- Scissors
- 50cm (20in) of 90cm (36in) wide fabric
- Scrap of contrasting plain fabric
- Dressmaking pins
- Iron
- Needle and matching thread

1 Transfer all the belt template pieces (page 123) to thin paper and cut out. Cut out all the belt pieces from the main fabric. Cut the lining for the side panels from the plain fabric. Pin one lining to one side panel and machine stitch together, right sides facing, using a 1cm (⅜in) seam allowance. Press open the seam. Repeat to join the other side panel to its lining. With right sides together, pin the side panels to the belt centre. Machine stitch together using a 1cm (⅜in) seam allowance.

2 Pin the straight ends of the of each tie to the ends of the side panels, with right sides facing. Machine stitch together, using a 1cm (⅜in) seam allowance. Press open all the seams. Fold the entire belt in half lengthways, right sides facing, pin and machine stitch the tie ends and lower edge using a 1cm (⅜in) seam allowance, leaving a 10cm (4in) opening in the lower edge to turn through.

3 Trim the corners of the tie ends and turn the belt through to the right side. Press under the raw edges of the opening and slip stitch closed. To add the quilted effect to the front of the belt, set your sewing machine to a medium straight stitch and sew rows of stitching along the belt centre, spacing them about 1cm (⅜in) apart.

Hip Hairband

Get it together...

- Thin paper and pencil
- Scissors
- Scrap of cotton fabric and matching thread
- Fusible interfacing
- Iron
- Dressmaking pins
- Needle
- 15cm (6in) length of 1.5cm (⅝in) wide elastic

1 Transfer the hairband templates (page 122) to thin paper and cut out. Cut a hairband front and back from fabric and one from interfacing, plus the hairband strap from fabric. Iron the interfacing to the wrong side of the hairband front. With right sides facing, pin and machine stitch the hairband pieces together using a 1cm (⅜in) seam allowance and leaving a 10cm (4in) opening along the lower edge to turn through. Trim the corners, then turn the hairband through to the right side. Press under the raw edges of the opening and slip stitch closed.

2 Press the hairband strap in half, right sides facing. Sew together down the long edge using a 1cm (⅜in) seam allowance. Turn through to the right side and press. Insert the elastic into the strap. Line up one end of the elastic with one end of the strap and machine stitch in place.

3 Press under the raw edges of the hairband sides. Insert and pin the sewn end of the strap into one end of the hairband front. Machine stitch over the join to keep the strap in place. Stretch the elastic to the other end of the strap. Line up the elastic edge with the strap edge, pin and machine stitch in place. Insert this end of the strap into the remaining end of the hairband and machine stitch over the join to secure.

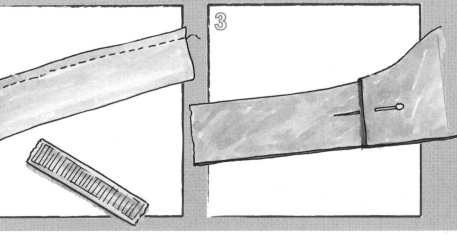

Get more...

Scrap Sense

» Any fabric scraps that you want to save for future use should be unpicked (unless any seams are worthy of reuse), washed and ironed flat. Remove usable zips or buttons and store them separately. Trim off any scrappy edges so that you have as large an area of fabric as possible. Make sure they are completely dry and aired, then store them, by colour, design or pattern, in clear plastic, lidded containers so that you can easily see what you've got. Keep a separate box of fabrics for linings and interlinings.

» Do you have some lightweight fabric that's too flimsy to make into a belt or a bag? Backing it with interfacing or interlining will make it sturdy enough to hold its shape. Interfacing is a washable material used to stiffen and strengthen fabric, which comes in different weights and in iron-on (fusible) or sew-in form. I use medium-weight fusible for bags, belts and cuffs, but the sew-in type for clothes, as I think it lays better. Interlining does the same job – simply a layer of stiffish fabric, such as twill or canvas, that you sew to the back of the fabric to be hidden by a lining before you make it up.

For an example of using interlinings, see the bag project on pages 104–110.

Cuff Couture

» If you're lucky enough to own a sequin foot, sewing the sequins onto the cuff will take you no time at all, although they won't work for individual sequins, only lengths of pre-sewn ones, available from craft suppliers. These sequins simply pop out through the adjustable front opening in the foot so that you can sew them directly onto the fabric. But if hand sewing, a good short cut is to attach each sequin with two running stitches before moving on to the next in the row.

» As an alternative decorative idea for your cuff, try machine appliquéing rows of ribbon across it, using a three-step zigzag stitch in a contrasting thread for an interesting effect.

Page 25 shows you what three-step zigzag stitch looks like and page 26 tells you more about it.

Scavenger Chic

» Men's ties are just perfect for making into hairbands, and there's no need to unpick them – just use the widest section and add elastic to the back. Also worth plundering are:
- cravats
- wide fabric belts
- square silk and long, narrow headscarves
- patterned woollen tights
- ribbed sections from the bottoms of sweaters

» If you come across a wide piece of fabric that you could use for the long, sash-style belt – such as a curtain of eye-popping florals – it would give you enough quantity to make it in one continuous piece. So, cut out all the pattern pieces, then tape them together, overlapping the seam allowances, to make one long pattern piece and cut out of the fabric on the fold in the usual way.

» If you're a really keen scavenger, you're bound to come across belt buckles on your forays, and you can reuse these to make fantastic belts speedily and easily. Just fold a long strip of a favourite fabric scrap into three (for extra body), turn under the raw edges and quilt it with close lines of machine stitching. Loop one end through the buckle and stitch in place. Make holes with an eyelet set, and voila, a new belt!

See pages 19–20 on what you need to fix eyelets.

Magic Makeovers

I'm usually good at getting rid of old clothes, but sometimes I find a piece of clothing whose colour or fabric is so fabulous that I can't bear to get rid of it. When this happens, I put it to one side, ready to be transformed into something new. This funky floral skirt started life as a smock top, but courtesy of my trusty sewing machine, a one-off design was soon created. To breathe new life into a second skirt, I simply added a narrow pleated edging in contrasting fabric around the hem.

Get into it...

Making full use of your zipper foot

I not only used this in the conventional way to sew in the zip at the side of the skirt but to attach the front pockets and to hem the bottom edge. This is because it enables you to sew very closely to the folded edge for a neat, finished effect.

 Interested in finding out about other gizmos for your machine? See pages 40–45.

Restyling with the right result

As I was going to make something completely new from an old garment, I used a paper pattern to ensure a really professional result and a good fit. You can buy clothes patterns from fabric shops, or look out for give-away ones from sewing magazines or download them free of charge from websites.

Saving on sewing

When cutting out the pockets for the skirt, I recycled the original hems by using them for the top edges of the pockets. Always look out for ready-hemmed edges on old garments that you can make use of in your restyled item, to save on your sewing time and effort.

Upcycling buttons

I've topped off the decoration on the pockets of my 'new' skirt with contrasting brightly coloured buttons, and used sewing thread in the buttonholes to match the pink of the ric rac trim for a coordinated look. The four-hole variety will give you the chance to sew a bold cross stitch in contrasting thread. Second-hand clothes are an ideal source of unusual buttons – garments that you may otherwise reject may have wonderful buttons, so grab them when you get the chance.

For tips on storing your buttons, braid and other decorative materials, see pages 100–101.

Pocket Panache

1 **To make the pockets**, fold your old item of clothing in half, right sides facing, and mark out a rectangle measuring 16.5 x 16cm (6½ x 6¼in), using the original hemmed edge for the pocket tops (the shorter edge) if possible. Cut out through both layers to make two pockets. Press under a 1.5cm (⅝in) hem at the sides and bottom of each pocket. Cut a length of ric rac to fit the top of each. Attach with a little fabric glue, then machine stitch in place with matching thread.

2 **To attach the pockets**, pin in place to the skirt front, spacing them evenly. Using the zipper foot and matching thread, machine stitch to the skirt, sewing as close to the pocket edge as you can. Sew a button to the centre of the top edge of each.

3 **To finish the skirt**, press under a narrow double hem around the lower edge and machine stitch in place, again using the zipper foot to get close to the folded edge. Add a trim of ric rac, as in Step 1. Press under the seam allowance at the side. Pin and tack (baste) the zip into the side seam, following your pattern instructions, then machine stitch in place using the zipper foot. Add a waistband according to your pattern and sew on a hook and bar fastening.

Get it together...

- Old item of clothing and matching thread
- Pencil and metal ruler
- Scissors
- 2m (2¼yd) ric rac and matching thread
- Fabric glue
- Dressmaking pins
- 2 buttons
- Iron
- 18cm (7in) skirt zip
- Tacking (basting) cotton and needle
- Skirt paper pattern
- Hook and bar fastening

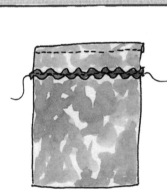

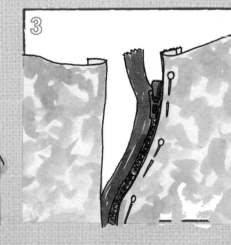

Neat Pleats

For this quick-and-easy makeover, measure around the hem of your old skirt and cut four pieces of 10cm (4in) wide fabric to that length. Pin the short sides together, with right sides facing, and machine stitch to join them into one long strip. **To pleat**, make a mark every 3cm (1¼in) along the strip top. Pinch the fabric at the first mark and pull it over to meet the third mark, then pin in place to form the first pleat. Repeat all the way along the strip. Hold the strip around the skirt hem to check that it fits. If it's too short, simply stitch more fabric onto the end and pleat it in the same way. **To secure the pleats in place**, machine stitch along the strip top about 1cm (⅜in) from the edge. Press the pleats to make them really sharp. Pin and tack (baste) the pleated strip around the skirt hem, on the right side, and machine stitch, using a 1.5cm (⅝in) seam allowance. **To cover the seam**, pin and tack (baste) cotton tape over the join, then machine stitch in place using your zipper foot and matching thread.

Get it together...

In addition to your usual sewing kit, not forgetting the old skirt itself, you'll need:
- 50cm (20in) of 90cm (36in) wide contrasting fabric and matching thread
- 1cm (⅜in) wide cotton tape to fit around the skirt hem

To smarten up a plain skirt still further, add a single pocket to the front (see page 77) and trim the top edge with a strip of the contrasting fabric used for the pleats.

Get more...

» When combining two or more garments, make sure that the fabrics are of the same type and weight so that they hang properly together and can be successfully laundered.

» Running short of fabric? Cut things like the waistband facings from a different fabric, as it won't show – no one will ever know!

» Do you have an old garment that you want to recycle and really like the design? Take a full-length photo of it and some details, then unpick it and make a paper copy of all the pieces so that you can use it again as a pattern.

» Think creatively about what ready-sewn features you can plunder from old garments. Smart cuffs and nicely gathered sleeves are great features, as well as contrasting pockets and any ruffles and frills that can be salvaged for trimming.

» Combine two different old items to make one new by:
· adding a **different skirt** to a **dress bodice**
· swapping the **sleeves** and **collars** of **two shirts**
· sewing a **man's waistcoat front** to the **back and sleeves** of a short **knitted cardigan** or **sweater**

» A great way to jazz up a jacket is to sew on a permanent corsage in contrasting but similar fabric. Appliquéd flowers, birds, spots, stripes or hearts would transform a plain shirt or skirt into a unique item (see above).

 For how to make a corsage, see page 58; for appliqué ideas, see pages 10–15.

» Want to spice up a plain skirt with a front pleat? Machine stitch a piece of brightly patterned fabric inside the pleat so that it flashes eye-catchingly when you walk.

» Headscarves offer bags of creative potential! Patterned retro examples make wonderful blouses (see left) – one scarf will usually give you enough fabric for the blouse fronts and short sleeves, and you can use a matching or contrasting scarf in a plain colour for the back. Headscarves are also great for making hairbands – choose the most interesting part of the scarf design for the front.

 Want to know how to make a hairband? See page 71 for some simple instructions.

GET THE MOST FROM... RECYCLING

Upcycled, recycled, thrifted, pre-loved, re-purposed — whatever you want to call it, sourcing and sewing with vintage materials is bang on trend. It seems everyone's realized that reusing fabrics is really cool and exciting, and your sewing machine may, in fact, help to save the planet!

Even mainstream fashion designers are getting in on the act, and the buzzword is upcycling — creating something new, funky and fabulous from an out-of-style, unloved garment. You will notice that I've salvaged many of the fabrics for this book from gorgeous bits and bobs I've found in flea markets, thrift stores and charity shops. Then I've whizzed into action with my sewing machine and executed a speedy makeover to transform them into new and covetable items. Clever design is the key here; no one wants a saggy tweed jacket, but re-cut it, change the buttons and stitch on a stylish new trim and you have a fashionista's dream at a fraction of designer prices.

www.recycling inspiration

If you're short on inspiring ideas for transformational sewing, the internet is awash with interesting websites that offer informative sewing tutorials and interesting patterns. They come and go, but some of my favourites are:

www.junkystyling.co.uk takes second-hand clothes and completely restyles them into cutting-edge designs.
www.traid.org.uk has a great fashion collection and 10 second-hand shops bursting with fabulous stuff.
www.craftster.org is an interesting website that serves the DIY sewing and craft communities.
www.threadbanger.com is a very hip DIY fashion and style website, offering loads of projects, tips, advice and news about fashion events.
www.fromsomewhere.co.uk is the website of a great London company that upcycles fabulous clothes from surplus designer fabrics such as swatches, ends of rolls and offcuts.

What to look for and where

Pillage your local second-hand shops, charity and thrift stores, car boot/yard sales and flea markets for old curtains, sheets, fabric remnants and clothes, looking for anything that catches your eye in terms of pattern, colour, texture, fabric quality and attractive ready-sewn features, such as pockets. But fabrics aren't the only materials ripe for recycling. Keep alert for interesting buttons and colourful zips, paper sewing patterns, reels of cotton and useful sewing notions, like hooks and eyes and other fastenings.

First steps with fabric finds

So, once you've gathered together your precious stash of pre-owned fabrics, before you start sewing them they may well be in need of a little TLC, so follow these preliminary steps to get them in shape for some upcycling action. Please note that as I prefer to sew with natural fibres like cotton and linen, the following washing instructions apply to these fabrics only.

1 It's important to check for moth damage when buying vintage fabrics – tiny holes nibbled into the fabric spell infestation, which means that you have to treat the fabric straight away with a moth deterrent before they invade your home!

2 Unpick items such as aprons, pillowcases and duvet covers to salvage as much of the fabric as possible. Remove the linings and headings from curtains. Remove any zips, elastic, fasteners, trims or buttons, then sort and store them if they can be reused.

3 Separate out any woollen fabrics such as tweed, as they need specialist cleaning attention. Curtains may also need specialist washing unless you're absolutely sure they're cotton and colourfast.

4 Don't be tempted to machine wash, spin or tumble dry obviously vintage fabrics at this stage, as they may be too delicate and you won't know whether they're colourfast. Gently handwash your fabrics in lukewarm water, rinse and air dry.

5 Large items such as sheets and duvet covers will have been through umpteen washes, so are safe to launder in the washing machine.

6 Iron your freshly washed fabrics and trim away any torn or holey parts, saving the largest area possible.

7 Fold your fabrics, wrap in tissue paper and store in open crates or baskets (to avoid getting musty), treated with a moth deterrent – you can now get non-chemical versions of the traditional camphor moth balls.

The machine magician

Now everything's washed and sorted, it's time to get your sewing machine set up and start sewing. Every kind and size of sewing project using your recycled fabric finds is just waiting for you to make it happen. You can create something from scratch – ranging from running up a quick cushion with the help of a gorgeous retro pillowcase to re-covering your sofa in stunning curtain fabric – or embellish existing items with creative trimmings and details to upcycle them into wonderful one-offs. In every case, your sewing machine is going to work its magic and make life a whole lot easier for you, and here's how...

Professional performance

The beauty of recycling fabrics with your sewing machine is that with a little thought and some serious attention to detail you can achieve a fantastically neat and professional finish that looks more designer than hippy. The accuracy and consistency of a sewing machine counteracts the salvaged, rough-around-the-edges feel of some old fabrics and trimmings and gives them a real facelift, which is what elevates recyling into upcycling. This is about transforming one or two fantastic, well-matched fabrics into something new, fresh and exciting with the aid of your machine and its wealth of professional functions, rather than slapping together odd fabrics in a mishmash of textures and weights. You want sharp seams? Try a touch of overstitching. Need extra buttonholes to transform the neckline of a boring jacket? Zap them to perfection with your buttonhole foot. You can also use your machine to insert a zip expertly into a furnishing fabric purse, gather up a ruffled edge evenly for a cushion cover made from a headscarf or sew a tough mail sack tote bag with a super non-stick foot.

Quick action

Your machine can whizz up long seams in next to no time, and overlock the edges with zigzag or overcast stitch to stop them fraying. You can add metres of ribbon in minutes and scatter sequins along the top of an old duvet cover. And hems are a cinch to stitch with blind hem stitch (see page 26), as I was pleased to discover, after having hemmed many pairs of curtains laboriously by hand!

A helping arm

Your machine will probably have a free arm – most do, and you will usually find it by removing the storage box from the front of your machine. It makes a great little platform that enables you to get much closer to the action while sewing tricky areas like corners or darn holes. It's an invaluable tool for a large job such as making a sofa or chair cover, as there are so many inaccessible areas to sew. It's also a real help when you're appliquéing vintage fabric patches to a leg or sleeve – simply slide the garment on and off for instant accessibility.

Alchemy for fabric scraps

One of my bugbears with vintage fabric is that you sometimes get only a tiny scrap of material, and its difficult to know what to do with it. One solution is to piece the scraps together using a ¼in quilting foot (see page 44) to create panels of recycled fabric before you start. Then you can use the panels to make all sorts of divine accessories with a cool, quirky style all of their own. Scrap purses, cushion covers, small children's clothes, hairbands and handbags all look great pieced from colourful fabric scraps.

Transforming tool

Your machine is an amazing means of embellishing something you've already got into a unique item. Machine embroidery is one of my favourite looks, and a well-placed embroidered graphic will transform a child's dress or a pair of boring old curtains in an afternoon. You can also embroider over the motifs on vintage floral fabrics, for instance, to give them a contemporary take.

All the fancy utility and decorative stitch functions on your machine (see pages 24–27) are a great way of embellishing your work, especially if you get really creative and use some of the fabulous threads available, such as metallics and variegated thread.

Cottons, wools and linens aren't the only materials you can reuse. If you're nosing around markets and charity shops, you're bound to come across a lot of articles made from leather and suede, which are perfectly straightforward to sew on your machine if you use the right needles and thread (see pages 62–63). Belts make great straps for bags made from any fabric and you can also create lovely appliqué patches and corsages from thin leather scraps.

Sample Sensation

Fabric sample books are a superb source of fabulous fabrics for sewing projects. These huge tomes are created by textile manufacturers to show customers all their fabric ranges and colourways, and are chock-full of fabric squares. The books go out of date at the end of each season, so you can get single samples for free, or nearly, from curtain and upholstery shops. I've also found the books in charity shops. From each fabric piece you can fashion a purse or even a bag. I've used 60s Swedish furnishing fabric to do just that here, which is both stunning to look at and very hardwearing.

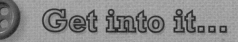
Finding a new use for old zips

While you're on the lookout for fabric samples, keep your eyes open for zips too – I bought a bundle of these brightly coloured ones in our local cat charity shop for less than the price of one new zip! Second-hand clothes are also a great source of zips, and if you've bought a garment to cut up and restyle, simply remove the zip before you begin. An 18cm (7in) skirt zip is perfect for this project. But if you can't find the right size, plastic zips can be trimmed to length: simply cut off the excess from the bottom and secure the ends together with a few stitches.

Want some more creative ideas and practical tips on recycling? See pages 80–83.

Contrasting creatively

For the belt feature on the front of the purse, I've used a strip of fabric with the same design but in a strongly contrasting colour for maximum impact – in fact, the complementary colour to that of the main fabric from the opposite side of the colour wheel, so it's guaranteed to look good! Other colour combos that would work equally well are:
• **purple purse** with a **hot pink** or **lime green belt**
• **navy blue purse** with a **light blue belt**
• **hot pink purse** with an **orange belt**
Alternatively, go for a **patterned purse** with a **plain belt** or vice versa.

Combining style with function

Although the machine stitching on the belt is functional (to hem the edges and secure the buckle in place), as is the top stitching either side of the zip (to reduce the amount of zip tape on show), it also adds another decorative dimension worked in a contrasting shade of the fabric colour. You can take this a step further with plain fabrics, using strongly contrasting thread that will

help to define the purse's shape. For example:
• hot colours like **pink, orange** and **lime** would look great with **navy blue thread**
• **red** is good with **light pink** or **white thread**
• **navy** is good with **pale blue thread**
• **dark blue** or **black thread** is a safe bet with most heavily patterned fabrics

Exploiting the fabric's features

I cut out the back of the purse from the fabric sample to make the most of the stylized flower motif, ensuring that it was positioned exactly in the centre. Different patterned fabrics may well offer other design features you can put to good use, such as incorporating the edge of a pattern into a border, or across the centre front of the purse to create an outline for the belt.

For more information on washing and storing vintage fabrics, see pages 81 and 100.

- Pencil and thin paper
- Scissors
- Fabric sample square, 40 x 40cm (16 x 16in), and contrasting and matching thread
- Contrasting fabric scrap for 'belt' and contrasting thread
- Buckle
- Iron
- Dressmaking pins
- Scrap of two different ribbons
- 18cm (7in) zip, in contrasting colour
- Tacking (basting) cotton and needle
- Metal split ring

1 Transfer the purse pattern twice to the fabric sample (page 124) for the front and back and cut out. Cut a strip of contrasting fabric to fit through the buckle. Press under a 1cm (⅜in) hem along each long edge and machine stitch in place with contrasting thread. Thread the strip through the buckle. Pin the strip to the purse front, overlapping the sides, then trim close to the sides. Machine stitch the sides of the strip to the purse front, using a 1cm (⅜in) seam allowance.

2 **To keep the buckle in place**, sew a line of top stitching down the contrasting strip to the left and right of it, then slide the buckle back to the centre of the purse. Fold a scrap of ribbon in half and pin to the right-hand side of the purse front just above the contrasting strip, with the loop pointing inwards. Machine stitch in place.

3 **To begin attaching the zip**, lay it face up on your table and pin the top of the purse front, face down, to the upper edge of the zip, lining up the raw edge with the top of the zip tape. Tack (baste) the zip in place and remove the pins.

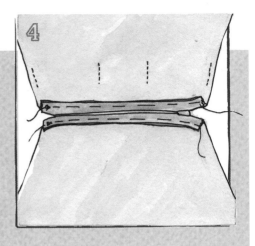

4 To finish attaching the zip, pin the top of the purse back to the lower edge of the zip, lining up the raw edge with the bottom of the zip tape. Tack (baste) the zip in place and remove the pins. Machine stitch both sides of the zip in place, then remove the tacking (basting) stitches. Place the purse right side up. Attach the zipper foot to your sewing machine. Open the zip halfway and top stitch along both sides of the zip, then close the zip again.

5 Pin the purse front and back together, right sides facing, along the sides and base. Machine stitch with matching thread, using a 1.5cm (⅝in) seam allowance.

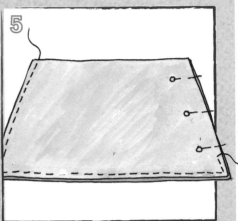

6 To finish making up the purse, press open the side and base seams, then press each corner flat so that the base and side seam are aligning and measure in 2cm (¾in) at either side. Mark a guideline across the base of the purse at each corner and machine stitch across. Trim the excess fabric. Turn the purse the right way out and press. Attach a split ring to the loop at the side, then thread the zip pull with a scrap of ribbon and tie in place.

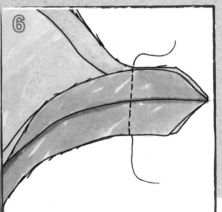

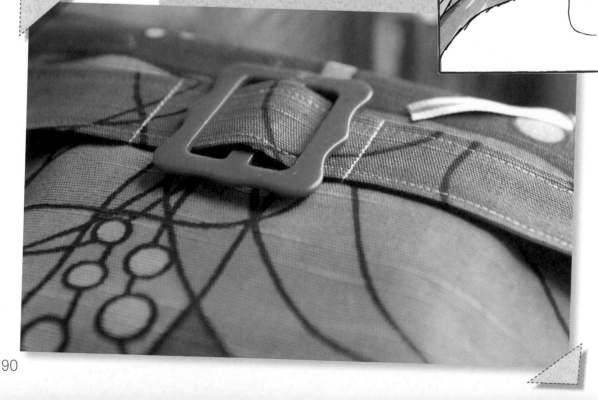

Get more...

» Some sewing machines don't have a separate zipper foot, but instead you'll be able to move the foot manually to the left and right, allowing you to stitch close to the zip in the same way. You can pass on top stitching the zip at Step 4 if you like; it just means that more of the zip tape will be visible.

» Some patterns are so stunning that they need no other embellishment, such as this explosive, abstract design, but if you can get the same fabric sample in a different colourway, use it for the back of the purse. In any case, a purse is a great way of using a small piece of fabric that you really love but is too small for anything else.

» To help you select the part of the fabric pattern that works the best, cut out the pattern shape from the centre of a piece of paper to make a frame. You can then move this over the fabric until you decide on the most effective 'crop'.

» For an alternative purse design, stitch together strips of fabric in different patterns but on a single colour theme, as above – furnishing fabrics are particularly rewarding for this treatment, as their large, powerful motifs look quite abstract and intriguing used in snippets. Choose the boldest for the centre to make a focal point and balance the composition around it.

» Why not get your machine into gear again to spice up your ribbon details and trimmings with some snappy stitching in a contrasting thread (see below) – oversize straight stitches, zigzag or any other fancy stitch on offer.

» Refine the basic purse design by adding some extra practical features:
• a **ribbon loop** inside for attaching a **key ring**
• using **plasticized fabrics**, such as **PVC**, to make the purse **waterproof** for containing **cosmetics**

» Try teaming up a patterned fabric for the purse with a front flap in a plain fabric, such as in the example pictured below. This way, the plain won't overpower the patterned but instead act as an effective contrasting background colour, emphasizing the design.

For some useful guidance on sewing through plastics and other unusual materials, see pages 60–65.

Mean Jean Machine

A cover is essential to keep your sewing machine clean and dust free. If yours doesn't have one, or is past its prime, grab some old jeans and make this stylistic version featuring a host of storage features. The waistband and belt tabs are reincarnated as handy holders for cotton reels, while the rest of the belt keeps a pair of scissors safely tucked away. Jeans pockets sewn to the front make clever containers for bobbins and packets of needles, and there's a zipped pocket on the back for your machine's manual.

Get into it...

Making to measure

Tailor-make the cover to your particular machine by measuring it at its highest and widest points to get the dimensions for the front and back, not forgetting to allow for a 1.5cm (⅝in) seam all round. Be sure to push down all the cotton reel holders before you begin. Most modern machines have slanted sides, so bear this in mind if you want to make a shaped cover. If not, measure across the sides at the widest points to make a basic rectangular cover.

Getting the most from your fabric

Seek out the largest-sized jeans possible to make the cover, because that way you'll get so much more denim for your money. I managed to cut the whole cover from one pair of jeans and added the details from two extra pairs. Using two or three pairs of old jeans in this way gives you the opportunity to contrast dark denim details against a paler, faded denim for the cover, as I've done here, or vice versa.

Reusing the stitching

I've tried to incorporate as many of the original seams from the jeans as possible. Placing the lower edges of the front and back and sides on a seamed edge not only looks good but it saves you having to sew hems through several layers of tough denim. I've also preserved as much of the original top stitching as I could by unpicking the pockets and waistbands carefully and then machine stitching them to the cover using blue thread so that the top stitching is still visible.

Preventing edges from fraying

It's essential to finish the edges of each piece of the cover neatly before you assemble them, because the denim will fray badly otherwise, tangling the threads as you sew. Use your machine's overlocking stitch, if you have one, or neaten the edges with a narrow zigzag stitch and trim away any stray threads.

See page 99 for more advice on storing and maintaining your trusty sewing machine.

For further information on overlocking, zigzag and the other stitches you can sew on your machine, see pages 22–27.

Get it together...

1 Transfer the heart template (page 124) to the paper side of the fusible webbing and roughly cut out. Place the cut-out, glue-side down, onto the back of a scrap of patterned fabric, iron over it to fuse it to the fabric and carefully cut it out. Remove the backing paper and position the heart on one of the denim pockets. Place a pressing cloth over the heart and iron over it to fuse it in place. Machine stitch around the edges in a fairly free way, using contrasting thread and a medium straight stitch. Machine stitch a line of narrow ribbon along the top of each pocket.

2 Measure your sewing machine to determine the cover dimensions (see opposite) and cut paper patterns for the front and back, sides and top pieces. Pin these to your denim and cut them all out. Unpick the waistband section. Cut the waistband into two pieces, press under the raw ends and pin to the cover front. Machine stitch in place using matching thread and following the original stitching lines. Repeat with the heart-decorated and second pocket. Pin the sides to the cover front with right sides facing. Machine stitch the seams to within 1.5cm (⅝in) of the top edge, using a 1.5cm (⅝in) seam allowance.

3 Press the cover top in half lengthways. Open it out and draw a 2cm (¾in) wide, narrow rectangle on the wrong side with a fine marker pen, long enough to accommodate your sewing machine's handle. Draw in cut marks, as shown in the illustration.

- Pencil and thin paper
- Scissors
- Fusible webbing
- Scraps of patterned fabric and contrasting thread and matching thread
- Iron
- Old demin jeans, including two pockets for the front cover and one for the back, and matching and contrasting thread
- Pressing cloth
- Narrow ribbon
- Measuring tape
- Dressmaking pins
- Fine marker pen
- Tacking (basting) cotton and needle
- Zip, as long as the width of the pocket (I used a skirt zip)

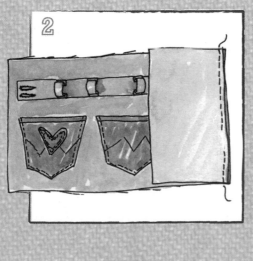

4 Snip along the cut marks with scissors. Press under the raw edges to the wrong side of the fabric to form the handle slot. Top stitch around the edges of the slot using contrasting thread.

5 Pin the cover top to the cover sides and front with right sides facing and matching the corners exactly. Machine stitch together, using a 1.5cm (⅝in) seam allowance, to within 1.5cm (⅝in) of the ends so that you can attach the cover back later. Pin and tack (baste) the lower edge of one side of the zip tape to the wrong side of the remaining pocket. Machine stitch in place using your zipper foot. Pin the pocket face down to the right side of the cover back, about 4cm (1½in) down from the top edge, and tack (baste) down the second side of the zip tape in place, then machine stitch using your zipper foot. Flip the pocket over to the right side, then pin and machine stitch around the edges using matching thread, following the original stitching lines.

6 Pin the cover back to the sides and top with right sides facing and matching the corners and edges exactly. Machine stitch all round, using a 1.5cm (⅝in) seam allowance. Trim the corners, turn through to the right side and press the seams open. Cut a 12cm (4¾in) wide strip of patterned fabric to fit around the lower edge of the cover. Press under and machine stitch a narrow 1cm (⅜in) hem down the long sides. Press the strip in half and pin to the cover lower edge, overlapping the raw short edges where they meet at the back. Using your zipper foot, machine stitch in place on the front of the cover so that you sew the top edge of the back of the strip to the reverse of the cover at the same time.

Get more...

» If you have an existing fabric or plastic cover for your machine, measure it to get the dimensions of your new cover, but don't forget to add a 1.5cm (⅝in) seam allowance to the sides, top and bottom of each piece. If your old cover is beyond use, carefully unpick it and use it to make a paper pattern.

» Can't bear to cut up your old jeans? Look out for a few old pairs from second-hand sources with interesting pockets and waistbands worth plundering. It's a good idea to ask your local charity shop staff if they have any really tatty pairs that they can't sell, which they'll often be glad to give away to a good home.

» Always use a denim needle when sewing jeans fabric, as they enable you to sew through all the layers of tough fabric with comparative ease. Stitch slowly though, because the needles will snap if you work too quickly, which is particularly annoying if you're in the middle of a seam!

See pages 60–65 for more tips on using different needles and thread for various specialist fabrics and other materials.

» Have fun adding different decorative details to the pockets like:
• **simple embroidery stitches** or **fancy stitches** on your **machine**
• **top stitching** over the original stitching with **brightly coloured thread** that complements the fabric colour
• **outlining** around the **pockets** with fancy **ribbon** or sparkling **sequins**

» Consider using other kinds of jeans for making the cover, such as:
• **plain cotton ones**, embellished with **extra appliquéd motifs**
• **needlecord jeans** for a more textured effect
• **border-style trousers**, which offer lots of **extra pockets, tabs** and **zips**, for a hardworking utility look

» Denim jeans and their features can be used in other unexpected ways, such as to make a new-look Christmas stocking (see left). Try to incorporate the original top-stitched seams to add visual interest and texture to the design, and jolly it up with a colourful patterned cotton fabric band at the top and an appliquéd festive motif.

» Large denim shirts or jackets will yield a wider expanse of fabric for reusing in larger projects, such as a bag (see right), and once you've removed the pockets, you can use the contrasting-toned patches as part of the design. A particularly attractive pocket makes a great focal point for the front of the bag, as well as having a practical purpose.

» Collect classic jean manufacturers' name tags and dot around your designs for an interesting effect.

GET THE MOST FROM...

Your WORKSPACE

And so to sew… but just how do you go about making the creative space of your dreams a reality? You may be lucky enough to commandeer a room for yourself, away from the hustle and bustle of everyday life, a space where you can close the door and work in peace. However, chances are that you won't, but there are ways of carving out a little haven for yourself from the smallest of spaces, perhaps in the corner of the sitting room or in an under-stairs area. All you need is a little forward planning and even the humblest of environments can become your very own personal studio, a sanctuary where you can play with your sewing machine to your heart's content.

The golden rule of a happy workspace, large or small

A place for everything, and everything back in its place when you've finished with it!

The result is that you will always be able to lay your hands on your tools and materials, and your workspace will stay organized. This is especially important if you have only a limited amount of time to spare for your sewing – you don't want to waste precious minutes hunting for your scissors or a packet of machine needles!

The engine of your workspace

If you can keep this central bit of kit, your sewing machine, near to hand and ready

to use at all times, so much the better. It will encourage you to use it and save you unpacking it every time you have a spare hour or two. Keep it covered when not in use (see pages 92–96 for how to make your own cover with storage features) so that it doesn't get dusty, and clean and oil it regularly, following the manufacturer's instructions.

Machine maintenance

Your machine should come with a manual and these few simple tools, so that you can keep it in good running order. But if you don't have these for any reason, you can buy them from your sewing shop or direct from the manufacturer:

- sewing machine oil
- brush to clean out lint and stray threads
- small screwdriver for minor adjustments

Your working surface

At the heart of every good workspace lies the surface that you work on. This should provide you with enough room to spread your work out, cut fabric and use your sewing machine all at the same time.

Choosing a table

A good old, family-sized kitchen table is great, but bear in mind that it will be relatively wide as well as long. Some people advocate using a computer table or small decorative desk for sewing, but I disagree; you're going to need as much surface area as possible to work on, so go for a long, flat surface every time, because switching between tables gets really annoying in the end.

Fitting a wooden or laminate surface

The joy of these work surfaces is that they can be cut exactly to size, to fit into the corner of a room or a space under the stairs, using up as much of the available space as possible. Widely available from kitchen stores and hardware stores or builders' merchants, they can be placed on trestle legs or fixed directly to the wall with wood or metal supports.

They are usually reasonably priced and they needn't be an eyesore – you can get laminated wood versions or even solid oak, although the latter are more expensive.

 Check out your local kitchen shop to see if they have any offcuts of work surfaces on sale for a reasonable price.

Smart shelving

This is another essential feature of the workspace. Shelves are particularly useful if you have a small area without much floor space, as they allow you to keep items off the floor and in a place where you can see them easily, and also to store stuff neatly that you don't often use until you want it.

Wall-mounted shelves

These can be cut to length for a perfect fit, and run across the entire length of the wall if you wish. If you position your work surface just beneath your shelves, you'll have instant access to all your everyday tools, fabrics and reference books.

 Make sure you fit wall shelves properly so that they are strong and secure enough to bear the weight of your items – there's nothing more alarming and frustrating than having all your precious jars and boxes come crashing to the ground!

Bookcases

These are great for slotting into a corner to maximize available space, and the top shelves are ideal for tucking away tools and materials that you don't often use.

See-through storage

There is a multitude of storage options on offer, but I go for those that reveal their contents at a glance.

Transparent plastic crates

I always use these to store my fabric stash because I am able to see what's in them without having to get them down off the shelf, which saves a lot of time. They also keep the fabrics neat and clean until I need them, and being open they prevent the fabrics becoming musty. Some come with rollers so that you can easily pull them out from under your work surface and push them in when you've finished with them.

Smaller plastic boxes

These are good for holding cotton reels, ribbons and other small items.

Clear glass jars

I use these to keep beads and sequins both safe and organized, and also because it's a pleasure to see their contents on display. Recycled screw-top jars are ideal.

Photo pocket display panels

For stylish high-visibility storage, fill the pockets of these display panels that hang on the wall with scissors, bobbins, cotton reels and so on, and you'll never have to spend ages searching for something again.

Second-hand storage

I believe the workspace should feast the eyes, so I scour charity shops and markets for lovely second-hand boxes and tins for storing small items such as buttons. Another good upcycling option is the humble wooden fruit crate. I beg these from my friendly greengrocer and use them to store jars of items I regularly use, like scissors, pencils and pins.

Ironing board and iron

These are vital items of equipment for the sewer. You will need to iron fabric before you cut it out, press open seams as you work and press under hems and turnings, as well as iron your finished garment.

Best board

Try to find a board with a well-padded ironing surface, or cover the top with a thin folded blanket and a cotton sheet to make a really smooth surface to work on.

If you're short of space, think about getting a tabletop ironing board, as these are much smaller than standard boards and take up far less room.

Iron right

I would recommend using a steam iron for sewing, as it's very difficult to get fabric completely flat using dry heat alone. But always make sure that the fabric you are using can stand steam and won't shrink in the process. Use a pressing cloth on delicate fabrics – a piece of plain white 100% cotton sheeting is perfect – to save marking them.

There are many proprietary cleaners available to spruce up your iron's pressing plate, but I find you can't beat a quick scrub with a pad of steel wool.

Safe seating

It's very easy to strain your back when you're sitting down sewing, so find yourself a good, supportive chair and you'll be able to work in comfort. The best choice is one adjustable in height with a backrest, enabling you to make it just the right height for your own work surface. Always try to sit with a straight back, and keep your chair pulled well under your table as you work.

To save eyestrain and to help you to sew straight, place your machine with the needle directly in front of you so that you can see both sides of the presser foot at once.

Lighting lesson

Sewing by daylight is the easiest on the eyes, but most of us have to grab a few hours whenever we can, so find ourselves sewing in the evening. If this sounds like you, invest in daylight bulbs, or have a small table lamp with a daylight bulb next to your machine.

R & R

Furnish your workspace with a radio or CD player to provide a relaxing atmosphere and make sure you have a facility for providing a refreshing drink on hand for those well-earned breaks.

Inspiration and instruction

Inspirational ideas and technical guidance are just as important in sewing as the nuts and bolts, and can come from a variety of sources, so think about how you might accommodate these in your everyday workspace.

Setting up a dedicated library

I'd be lost without my books. They provide me with inspiration, show me how to do things properly and console me when a project's gone wrong. Place a comfortable chair in a corner, if you've got the space, and keep your books next to it on a dedicated shelf or small bookcase so that you can sit down and really concentrate on what you're reading. An overhead lamp will make reading a lot easier and give your corner a warm and inviting glow.

Compiling cuttings

I also keep folders of pictures from magazines, postcards, giftwrap and anything else that catches my eye and might inspire me in the future. It's a good idea to have several folders if you've got lots of cuttings, and arrange them by subject or technique, to help you find what you're looking for quickly and easily.

Creating a mood board

The walls of my work room are peppered with bits and pieces cut from magazines, pictures that inspire me, tiny pieces of trim, scraps of interesting fabric, buttons, telephone messages and so on. At one time they threatened to completely engulf the room, but nowadays I keep them all in one place for easy access on a fabric-covered cork noticeboard, where they also make a great focal point. If you've generated a wealth of such sample material, consider covering a section of your wall with a panel of self-adhesive cork tiles for the ultimate pinboard.

Plastic Fantastic

I designed this little photo bag with fun in mind, and to show you how easy it is to sew plastics. It might seem weird to deliberately put plastic on your bag, when we're trying so hard to stop using the stuff. However, when you discover that it's just one of the many alternative materials your sewing machine can tackle, it's just too tempting to resist.

Get into it...

Sewing through plastic

This is so easy with a sewing machine, giving crisp, durable results. Once you've tried it for the first time, you'll be looking around to see what else could benefit from a plastic pocket!

> Pages 60–65 offer more information on sewing through unusual materials.

Looking for unlikely fabric sources

My local flea market revealed a very worn apron made from gorgeous 50s folk-art fabric. It had a big hole in the middle, but there was a nice large panel at the bottom still intact.

> See pages 80–83 for tips on recycling.

Adding quick-change elements

Knowing how quickly I get bored with things, I decided to add the plastic photo pocket to the bag front so that I can show off a new photo every day, depending on my mood and what I've dug out of the giant cardboard box I call my photo album!

Mixing contrasting materials

Gorgeous shabby chic fabrics and quirky dark folk art don't seem obvious bedfellows, but mixing up your materials like this produces interesting results even on the plainest of projects. Mix and match some fabrics from your stash to find interesting pairs, for example:

• **smooth satin** emphasizes the texture of **frayed denim**

• **dark cord** toughens up pretty **pastel florals**

• **modern fluorescent pinks** and **yellows** are tamed by textured **natural linens**

- Pencil, ruler and thin paper
- Scissors
- Dressmaking pins and needle
- 30cm (12in) of 90cm (36in) wide fabric for the bag front and back
- 30cm (12in) of 90cm (36in) wide fabric for the linings
- 30cm (12in) of 90cm (36in) fabric for the interlinings
- scrap of contrasting fabric for the bottom band
- 12 x 18cm (4½ x 7in) plastic photo pocket and contrasting thread
- Low-tack sticky tape
- 1m (1¼yd) cotton tape
- Ric rac and matching thread
- Fabric glue
- Scrap of ribbon
- Metal split ring
- Photo

1 Transfer the bag templates (page 125) to thin paper to make a pattern. Cut a front and back from the main fabric, two linings and two interlinings. Pin the interlinings to the wrong sides of the bag front and back and machine stitch them in place, using a 1.5cm (⅝in) seam allowance.

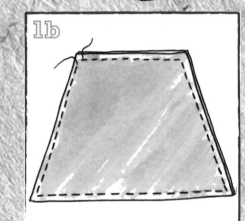

2 Cut a piece of contrasting fabric for the bottom band, the width of the bag bottom and about a third of the depth. Pin the band in place on the right side of the bag front and trim away the excess fabric. Stitch the fabric in place, lining up the side of the presser foot with the edge of the fabric.

3 Cut out a plastic photo pocket and attach it to the front of the bag with low-tack sticky tape (my photo pockets came in a sheet of four). Stitch around the sides and base of the pocket in contrasting thread, removing the tape before you reach it. Pull the threads to the back of the fabric and tie off the ends.

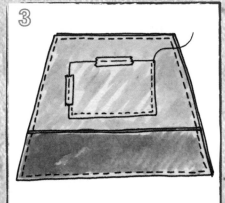

4 **For the handles,** cut the cotton tape into two equal lengths. Pin the handles to the bag front and back, lining up the ends of the tape with the top of the fabric, and stitch in place. Your machine will sew a strong bond to ensure handles that can carry any load (even if you can't!).

5 **To add the contrast trims,** cut a length of ric rac to fit across the bag front and back a short distance from the top edge. Machine stitch in place with matching thread. Cut a 7cm (2¾in) length of ribbon, fold in half and pin to the right-hand side of the bag to make a loop. Stitch in place.

6 **To start sewing the bag together,** with right sides facing, pin the front and back of the bag together. Machine stitch around the sides and base of the bag, using a 1.5cm (⅝in) seam allowance. Pin and sew the two lining pieces together in the same way.

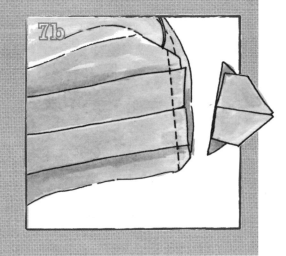

7 **To create a flat base,** press open the side and base seams. Press each corner flat so that the base and side seam are aligning and measure in 3cm (1¼in) at either side. Mark a guideline across the bag base at each corner with a ruler and pencil and machine stitch. Trim the excess fabric. Do the same with the bag lining.

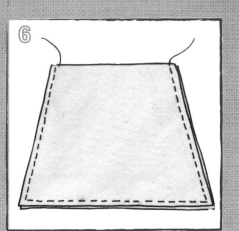

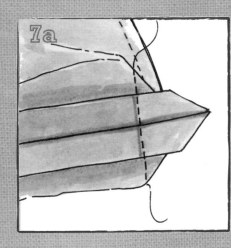

8 To attach the lining to the bag, first turn the bag through to the right side and press. Pull the lining, wrong side out, over the bag and pin the two together at the top edge, matching side seams. Make sure the handles are between the bag and lining, then machine stitch around the top edge, using a 1.5cm (⅝in) seam allowance and leaving a 10cm (4in) gap along the back edge. Turn the bag and lining through to the right side.

9 To complete the bag, push the lining down into the bag. Press under the raw edges of the opening along the top edge. Slip stitch the opening closed. Attach a metal split ring to the loop at the side of the bag and insert a photo into the pocket.

I add a tab and ring to all my bags and purses – they're so handy for attaching keys, charms and even other purses! Turn to page 91 to see other examples.

Get more...

» I used a plastic photo pocket for the front of this bag. You can get them from photographic suppliers or online, but don't worry if you can't find any – use a piece of clear acetate cut to size instead.

» Sticky tape is a brilliant alternative to pins when working with plastic. Choose the low-tack variety to make it easy to peel off – especially important, as you need to do this just before your sewing machine needle reaches it.

» If you don't want to see the plastic's raw edges, try using one of your machine's decorative stitches to disguise them.

Find out more about fancy machine stitches on pages 25–27.

» This bag makes the perfect present for a friend – surprise them by including a photo from a long-forgotten party, memorable childhood moment (see above!) or to reflect their favourite hobby. It's the ultimate personalized gift.

» If you've been good and have been using sustainable fabric bags instead of plastic bags over the past few years, the handles might be looking a bit tatty. Unpick the stitching, remove the tired old handles and replace them with funky new ones. It's quick and easy to make your own using your sewing machine and strips of fabric.

» Ric rac is a totally versatile trim and perfect for machine stitching. Indulge your material-girl side and choose stripes of clashing modern and retro fabrics that can be interspersed with the vintage-look ric rac (see the variation on the bag design, right).

» Sewing on ric rac can be a bit tricky, so dab a little fabric glue on the back of the it first to anchor it while you sew. Make sure you let it dry before it comes into contact with your machine needle.

Photo Finish

Paper has a similar weight and feel to fabric, comes in an array of mouth-watering colours and patterns, and can likewise be stitched on your machine. I made these fun greetings cards in a single afternoon, some using basic card and decorative printed paper; others sheets of magical fabric on which you can print out your favourite images from your computer just like paper! I then enjoyed transforming them into something fresh and arty using machine stitching and other embellishments as an integral part of the design.

Get into it...

Sewing with paper

The key to success when machine stitching paper is to choose the right weight of paper and the right needle and thread for the job (see page 62). Stick flimsy decorative papers to a sturdier backing paper or card before you start stitching, such as I've done here with the Fancy Footwork photo (see below), otherwise you run the risk of tearing the delicate surface as the needle goes through it. Once you've done this simple preparation, you can sew paper in exactly the same way as fabric, using all the decorative and fancy stitches your machine has to offer.

> Fancy trying your hand at sewing other more unusual materials? See pages 60–65 for ideas and practical hints and tips.

Choosing the right card

For the base cards, I have used A4 (US letter) sheets of card folded in half, but you could use pre-cut card blanks instead. Bear in mind, though, that whether you decide to buy or make your own blanks, don't choose card any heavier than medium weight, or about 300gsm, otherwise you'll find it tricky to sew. Envelopes come in standard sizes, so if you do make your own blanks of a size other than the one I've specified here, make sure you can find an envelope in the same size before you begin.

Being clever with your photos

Look through your collection of family photos and choose those with bright colours and striking, dynamic images. For the paper card designs, I printed my photos from my computer onto ordinary photographic paper, then stitched them directly to card, or paper-covered card. Choose these in a colour that contrasts with the photo but picks up on a colour that features in the image – the pumpkin card's two-tone design, for instance, has real wow factor. For the fabric designs, the printable fabric comes in A4 (US letter) sheets. Once processed, you simply remove the backing to reveal your own unique cotton fabric, printed with the image of your choice. You can machine or hand sew this in any way you please, so it's great for adding buttons and ribbons as embellishment, then machine stitch it to a pre-cut card blank.

Stitching in style

Don't just stitch timidly around the edges of your photos; think about the subject matter and try to match your sewing style to what's in the picture. For the pumpkin card, I sewed uneven rows of black stitching to create a scratchy, scribbled look that reflects the nerve-tingling, spooky atmosphere of Halloween. The picture of the bowling shoe-clad feet, on the other hand, is fun and informal, so I zigzagged around it with bright pink thread, then added a little frivolous stitched heart to one corner.

> See pages 22–27 for information on the different stitches you can do on your sewing machine.

- A4 (US letter) sheets of coloured medium-weight card and coordinating and contrasting threads
- Pencil and metal ruler
- Craft knife and cutting mat or scissors
- Decorative printed paper
- Paper glue
- 15 x 10cm (6 x 4in) photos

Fancy Footwork

Fold a sheet of card in half. Using a craft knife with a metal ruler and working over a cutting mat or using scissors, trim it down to make a landscape-shaped folded card (with the fold at the top) measuring 13 x 18cm (5 x 7in). Cut a piece of printed paper to fit the front and stick in place with paper glue. Glue your photo centrally to the front. Machine stitch a line of straight stitches around the card using coordinating thread, about 5mm (³⁄₁₆in) from the edge. Switch your machine to zigzag and sew several times around the edges of the photo. Switch your machine back to straight stitch and sew a small heart in the bottom left-hand corner of the photo.

Jack-O' in Stitches

Prepare the base card as for Fancy Footwork. Glue your photo to the front with paper glue, about 1cm (³⁄₈in) below the top edge. Thread your machine with contrasting thread and carefully stitch around some areas of the image, in this case the jack-o'-lantern's features. Switch to another thread colour and machine stitch around the edges of the photo, to make extra secure, then sew heavily around the card borders to make a dense, scribbled frame.

Festive Framing

Prepare the base card as before. Turn it upright and glue your photo centrally to the front. Thread your machine with contrasting thread. Sew around the edges of the photo, then around the card borders with two or three rows of stitching. Finish by sewing several rows of stitching across each corner.

Get it together...

- Photos
- A4 (US letter) sheets of printable fabric
- Scissors
- Beads, sequins, buttons and needle
- Narrow ribbon and braid and contrasting thread
- A4 (US letter) sheets of medium-weight card
- Scraps of printed fabric and matching thread
- Iron

Bubble and Bling

Print out your image onto a fabric sheet, following the manufacturer's instructions. Remove the backing paper once the ink has dried and trim away the excess fabric. Sew little beads onto your image to embellish it, in this case around the little girl's necklace, then add a few sequins for extra sparkle. Trim your image into a square and machine stitch it to a piece of folded card about 2cm (¾in) larger all round than your fabric. Cut a length of narrow ribbon and braid to fit two sides of the card and machine stitch around the edges of your image. Hand sew a button to the centre of the bottom edging.

Picture Patchwork

1 Prepare the fabric-printed image as for Bubble and Bling. Trim a scrap of printed fabric to the same width as your image and machine stitch the two pieces together, with right sides facing. Press open the seam.

2 Cut two strips of scrap fabric to fit either side of the picture panel and machine stitch the two pieces together, with right sides facing. Press open the seams.

3 Hand sew a few buttons along the middle seam. Machine stitch the panel to a piece of folded card, then sew lengths of narrow ribbon around the edges.

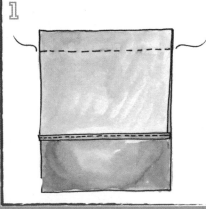

Get more...

» Pre-cut card blanks come in all sorts of wonderful shapes and sizes, so look at the variety available to get some inspiration for your card designs:
• **oval**, **rectangular** or **circle apertures** cut into the front to match the design of your **artwork** that you can attach behind
• a **row of three apertures**
• **four apertures** together like a **window frame**

» Or for a truly original result, try cutting your own aperture into a pre-cut blank, such as:
• a simple **tree shape** for a **Christmas card**
• a **heart-shaped aperture** for **Valentine's Day**

» Don't forget that you can stitch paper on the machine without any thread to create a delicate pattern of perforated holes, which you can feature as part of your designs. For example, try stitching a small photo in the centre of a card, then add a pricked paper border all round by stitching about 5mm (³⁄₁₆in) away from the edge of the photo.

 For an example of the paper-pricking effect, see page 62.

» Experimentation is the name of the game when you're sewing with paper. Try to hunt down exotic, handmade papers as well as the more everyday variety. Those from Japan, India and Nepal are very exciting, and may look extremely flimsy and unsuitable for sewing. But as they are hand laid using very long plant or rag fibres, they are actually incredibly strong and are rather like sewing fine cotton fabric.

» You don't have to buy expensive handmade papers to have fun with your designs:
• **Newspaper** (especially the **coloured variety**) is fantastic to sew, especially if you can find the crisp, broadsheet type
• **Giftwrap** is a great source of highly decorative (and free) paper (see above), and its lovely to sew, so start saving it now!
• **Food labels**, **magazines** and **decorative wallpapers** are other good sources of interesting and colourful printed papers

» Use different-sized card blanks and photos to make interesting compositions. For example, a small square photo stitched in the top left-hand corner or in the centre of a much larger square card looks great, especially if you add interesting effects to the background paper, such as heavy overstitching.

» If you've got lots of little scraps of paper, use them to make an interesting background for your photos by creating an eye-catching collage with them. Cut a piece of backing paper the same size as the front of your card blank, then add spots, stripes or blocks of coloured and patterned paper and machine stitch them all in place. Add your photo on top and embellish in the usual way.

GET THE MOST FROM...

Beyond Your WORKSPACE

Out there, beyond the confines of your sewing workspace, is a vibrant sewing community that you can tap into at the touch of a keyboard just waiting for you to join in all the fun. Blogs are the best way to connect with these like-minded souls, because you can interact with the authors and find wit, wisdom, sewing patterns, hints, tips and advice to boot. If you're feeling completely inspired by sewing, you might want to take the plunge and have a go at selling your own work, and again the internet is the answer, offering you access to a global audience, with many of its members into handmade goods. At the same time, you can keep up with the latest developments in the world of sewing by going to trade and craft fairs, sharpening up your skills on a short course and enjoy sharing your stitching savvy at a sewing get-together.

Entering the blogosphere

Creative people love writing blogs because creating can be a lonely business and blogging is a fantastic outlet for sharing thoughts, getting feedback on new designs and passing on snippets of advice and gossip, as well as connecting with kindred spirits.

Tapping into existing blogs

One of the best ways to see just who is out there in the blogosphere is to check out the many sewing blogs already in existence. To enter this magical world of creativity, just type 'sewing blogs' into your search engine and your computer will come up with a long list of really fascinating and beautifully illustrated blogs for you to peruse.

You're bound to get seriously addicted to reading blogs, so if you find one that you particularly like, sign up to follow it and you'll be automatically alerted to postings when the author writes something new. There will also be a feature that lets you leave comments for the author to read. This is another great way to network and share thoughts with the online sewing community.

Starting your own blog

• If you fancy having a go at blogging – and who doesn't – there are plenty of free sites to get you started. Simply sign up, choose your layout template, pick a font and off you go.

• The site I chose for my blog is Blogger, which is free to join, has great layouts and is extremely easy to use. Other good sites include Wordpress and Typepad. You can upload as many pictures as you like, to fit your chosen template, and there are also list-making facilities and interesting visuals for you to download.

• You can blog about anything you like; it doesn't all need to be about sewing. Some of my favourite blogs contain musings on everyday life or what it is to be creative, and insight into the blogger's lifestyle and family.

Four steps to blogging brilliance

It's a bit nerve-wracking when you first start a blog, as you do wonder whether people will see it or whether anyone will know you're there. The answer is yes they will, eventually – you just need to do the networking...

1 I find the best way to generate traffic to your site is to leave comments on other people's blogs, with a link to yours. Bloggers are curious and they will nearly always visit yours and leave a comment too.

2 The other bloggers may add your blog to their list of links so that their followers can visit you, generating loads of comments in a very short space of time.

3 Remember to post PLENTY of photos on your blog – the more the better – so that people can see your latest creations and give you feedback. You'll need a digital camera to do this and some software that lets you tweak the colour balance in your pictures.

4 Once you've posted your pictures, consider joining an online photo-sharing site such as Flickr. Here, you can upload your pictures (so you don't use tons of memory storing them on your computer) and submit them to groups (or pools) of pictures. This is another great way of networking, as you'll get comments from other pool members, and your work may even be spotted and blogged by someone else.

My top ten blogs

The following are some of my favourite blogs, just for starters:
* angry chicken
* HELLO my name is Heather
* ThreadBanger
* Sew, Mama, Sew!
* Frilly Bits
* make grow gather
* sandra juto
* Scherenschnitte
* The Sartorialist
* The vintage magpie

Selling online

You may only be interested in a part-time venture to generate extra income, or have ambitions to make it as an entrepreneur with a successful small business. Either way, nowadays it's simple to sell your handmade creations online and completely thrilling the first time you close the deal.

Doing your research

In the interests of market research, it's a good idea to try selling to family and friends first and to sample local craft and design fairs to check out whether your products and prices are appropriately pitched. This will also allow you to network with other local designers and makers, and put you in touch with an existing creative community. Once you've tested the waters, you'll know whether you want to make the leap to the internet with its worldwide customer base and sell online.

Dedicated arts and crafts marketplaces

Until recently, there were only two options for people wanting to sell their handmade goods online. One was to start a website, with all the hassle and expense of keeping it running smoothly while trying to drive customers to the site. The other was to join millions of other sellers on eBay, a general marketplace for new and second-hand goods.

Then, in 2005, Etsy, an online marketplace specifically designed to sell the work of artists and craftspeople, was founded in Brooklyn, New York. With low rates of commission, a great marketing team, lots of helpful advice on how to achieve sales and forums bursting with info from other sellers, Etsy quickly became super popular, and the number one spot for the discerning buyer and seller of handmade goods.

Advertised as 'a place to buy and sell all things handmade', it has a really simple and pain-free shop set-up and individual email addresses for sellers. There is enormous freedom to create a sophisticated and unique look for your shop and it's a cinch to list items for sale, so you can be up and running

in just a few hours. However, because of its vast popularity and having so many sellers, there's a danger of your work getting totally lost in the crowd. But increasingly there are more online sites where you can buy and sell your work, trade materials and advice, swap information and technical tips and tap into the worldwide design community – see below.

Top five arts and crafts marketplaces

Etsy	Folksy
Dawanda	Misi
Coriandr	

---

10 good reasons to open a shop at an online marketplace

1 You'll get loads of feedback about your work from other sellers via the site's craft forums.

2 You can test the water with your products for just a small financial outlay.

3 You can make and sell goods from the comfort of your own home – no more draughty craft fairs on rainy afternoons!

4 You'll be reaching a global audience, and far more people than you ever could through a traditional shop, at a fraction of the price.

5 It's really easy to set up an online shop and you'll get help and support from the administrative staff.

6 You'll only pay a very small commission to the site's hosts if you sell something. Some traditional galleries and shops charge more than 50% commission on sales, or mark up your wholesale prices so much that they end up taking more profit than you.

7 The host site will already have a ready-made customer base, so you won't be completely on your own, although you will have to do some serious self-promotion.

8 The forums are a great place to get information about materials, suppliers, commissions and buyers.

9 The site's hosts will be doing plenty of PR on your behalf, such as placing features in magazines and advertising online.

10 It's a great showcase for your work, introduces you to the global sewing community, lets you make lots of new friends and may even get you discovered by a magazine, a publishing house or a buyer from a big store!

All the fun of the fair

Trade fairs, exhibitions and craft fairs offer a feast of opportunities for the famished sewer, as outlined below, even if a trip to one of the massive, regular trade and consumer shows, staged in an exhibition hall or convention centre, can be an exhausting and foot-crippling marathon.

* There'll be literally hundreds of designers, materials suppliers and magazine and book publishers just waiting to meet you and give you the low-down on the latest trends.

* You'll come away hugely inspired by the fantastic fabrics that are available and the exciting range of techniques that you never even knew existed.

* You'll find most of the big sewing machine manufacturers at exhibitions like these, and they will be only too happy to demonstrate all the fabulous things that their machines do, so you can see all their snazzy functions in action first hand.

* A visit to a trade fair is a great day out and will be a real boost to your creativity, sending you down paths you never dreamed of, such as selling your own work.

* Craft fairs are showcases for designers and makers to exhibit and sell their latest work, and will put you in touch with local creative people. They may feature the very latest, cutting-edge products from established designers, or alternatively be low-key affairs where local sewing groups sell their goods on a regular basis.

* As well as offering a great opportunity to network and exchange ideas with fellow crafters, you'll also be able to find out about craft classes and workshops in your local area that you may fancy signing up for.

Back to school

Whatever your level of ability, its definitely worth brushing up your sewing skills at a workshop or on a short course. Here, experts will guide you through such specialist areas as tailoring and pattern cutting, or just focus on getting the dressmaking basics right, like layout and fabric cutting, reading a pattern, making tucks and pleats and so on. This can improve your sewing no end and help you to achieve really professional results.

Sewing and socializing

One of the best things about sewing is that it's a really sociable pastime. Way before the era of stitch 'n' bitch, groups of women got together to create the Bayeux and Cluny tapestries, and more recently fabulous friendship quilts. I'm not suggesting you form a quilting bee, but once you've got to grips with all the handy features on your sewing machine, why not share them with friends at your own workshop evening? Pick a simple project that showcases one function, such as inserting a zip or making a buttonhole, lay on a few snacks and drinks, then take turns to whip up a masterpiece on your sewing machine. This is a really great idea if you're preparing for a special event like a wedding or Christmas fair and you'll have hours of fun creating, swapping fabric, choosing patterns and picking up sewing tips.

Our grandmothers discovered the benefits of the 'sewing circle' during the era of make do and mend, and now it's the turn of our generation, so long may it continue!

Templates

Scrap Style, pages 66–73

Hip Hairband

place on fold

hairband front and back
cut 1 from interfacing
cut 2 from fabric

hairband strap
cut 1 from fabric

place on fold

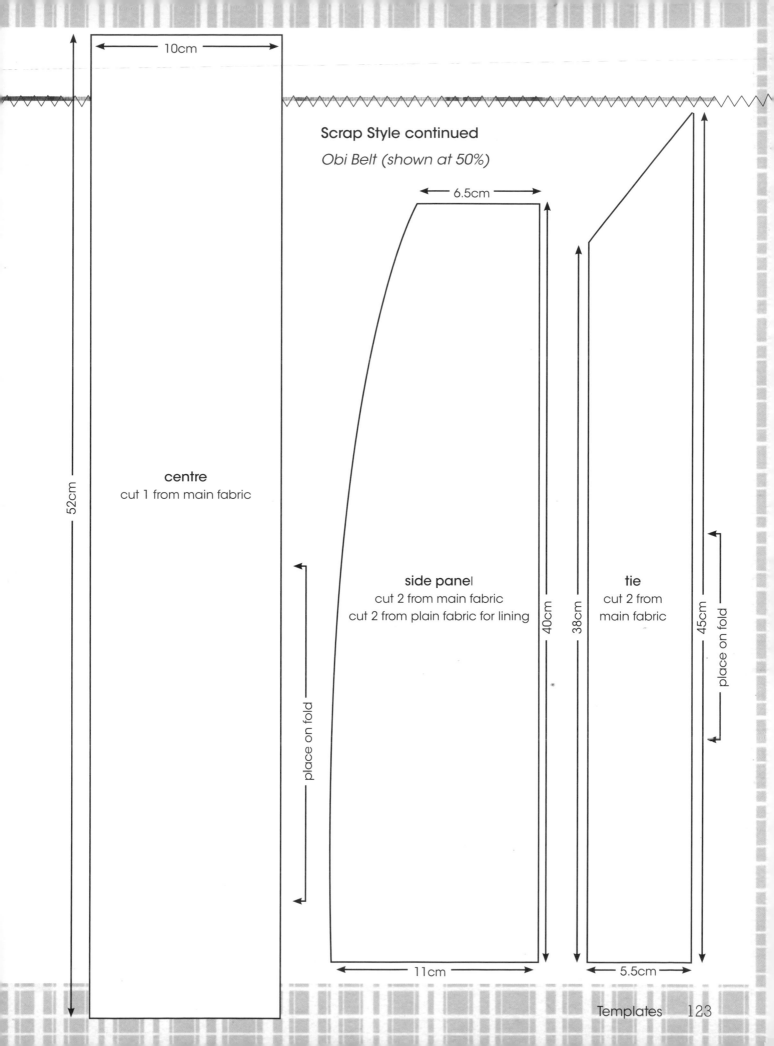

10cm

52cm

centre
cut 1 from main fabric

place on fold

Scrap Style continued

Obi Belt (shown at 50%)

6.5cm

side panel
cut 2 from main fabric
cut 2 from plain fabric for lining

40cm

11cm

38cm

tie
cut 2 from
main fabric

45cm

place on fold

5.5cm

Corsage Craft, pages 48–53

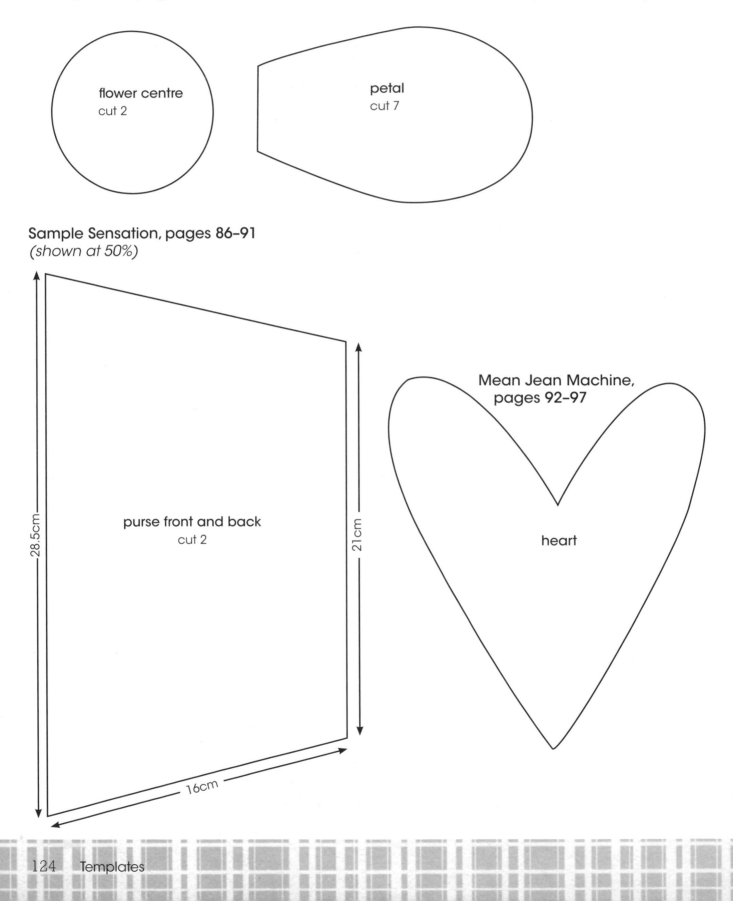

flower centre
cut 2

petal
cut 7

Sample Sensation, pages 86–91
(shown at 50%)

28.5cm

21cm

purse front and back
cut 2

16cm

Mean Jean Machine,
pages 92–97

heart

Plastic Fantastic, pages 104–111

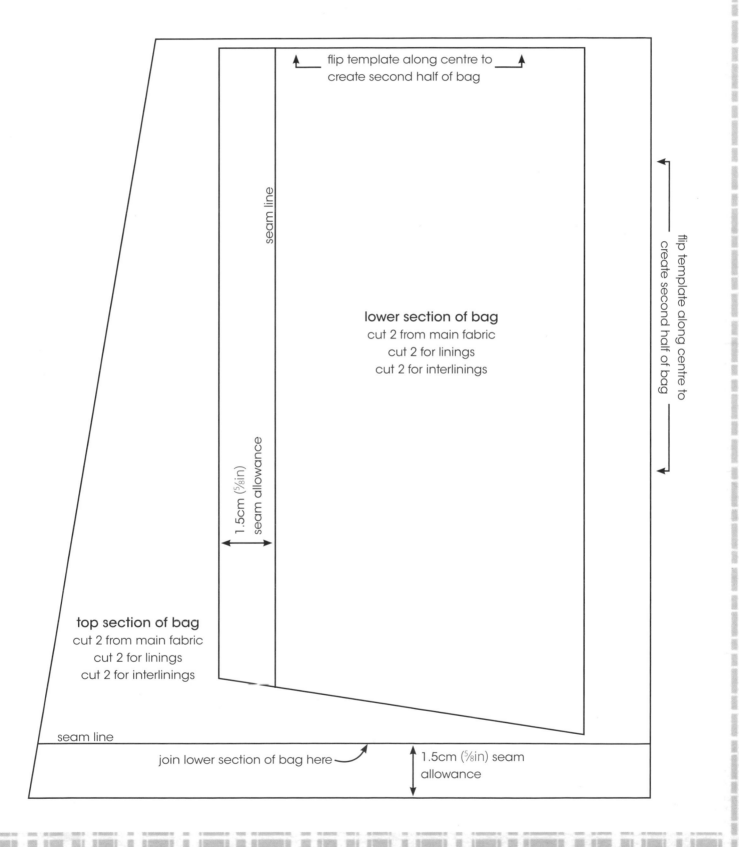

flip template along centre to create second half of bag

flip template along centre to create second half of bag

seam line

lower section of bag
cut 2 from main fabric
cut 2 for linings
cut 2 for interlinings

1.5cm (⅝in) seam allowance

top section of bag
cut 2 from main fabric
cut 2 for linings
cut 2 for interlinings

seam line

join lower section of bag here

1.5cm (⅝in) seam allowance

Suppliers

Brother International
www.brother-usa.com/homesewing
Tel: 1-908-704-1700
Leading manufacturer of sewing and embroidery machines

Chawla's
www.efabrics.co.uk
Tel: 0208 572 2902
Fantastic range of reasonably priced plain and patterned cotton fabrics and haberdashery trimmings

Donna Flower
www.donnaflower.com
Great collection of vintage and new fabrics for sale, as well as vintage buttons, ribbon and other trimmings

Doughty's, Hereford
www.doughtysonline.co.uk
Tel: 01432 267 542
Three great shops, stocking fabrics, haberdashery and patchworking materials

www.etsy.com/shop/ thisandthatfromjapan
Lovely fabrics and sewing books direct from Japan

www.misformake.co.uk
Beautiful and unusual Japanese cotton fabrics and sewing books

Reprodepot
www.reprodepotfabrics.com
Vintage reproduction fabrics, ribbons, buttons and other haberdashery supplies

Sewing Machines Direct
www.sewingmachines.co.uk
Freephone 0800 092 52 15
Suppliers of machines and attachments for all major brands

Truro Fabrics
www.trurofabrics.com
Tel: 01872 222 130
A wonderful shop with a vast array of dress and furnishing fabrics, trims, buttons, threads, paper dressmaking patterns etc.

Warm Biscuit Bedding Co
www.warmbiscuit.com
Toll-free tel: 800-231-4231
Brilliant collection of repro vintage fabrics; lovely children's designs

About the Author

Marion Elliot is a craft designer and author of more than 20 books, specializing in textile and paper crafts. She lived for many years in London, working as an art director and stylist, before escaping to the wilds of rural Shropshire in England. She now runs her own company, Vintage Town, selling an eclectic range of home accessories such as bags, tea cosies and purses, all made from vintage fabrics that she has collected and scavenged through the years. She has two online shops where you can buy her work, *www.folksy.com/shops/vintagetown* and *www.etsy.com/shop/vintagetown* as well as a blog at *www.vintagetown.blogspot.com*

Acknowledgments

I would like to thank everyone who has made this book possible. Among them, Jennifer Fox-Proverbs for knowing that sewing machines are really exciting, Stella for providing the beautiful artwork for the duvet set (left), Neil and Stella for taking lots of days out so that I could make things, my mum for letting me use her sewing machine all summer long and giving me such fantastic remnants, Sally for allowing me to borrow her camera for months on end, Wendy for looking enthusiastic about designs, Mia Farrant for being such a great model and for pulling it all together with her fab layouts and of course Jo Richardson for kindly and patiently keeping the whole show on the road.

Index